Jane Fonda
Cooking for Healthy Living

RECIPES
Robin Vitetta

PHOTOGRAPHS
Joyce Oudkerk Pool

ILLUSTRATIONS
Jennie Oppenheimer

PAVILION

First published in Great Britain in 1996 by
PAVILION BOOKS LIMITED
26 Upper Ground
London SE1 9PD

The moral right of the author has been asserted.

A CIP catalogue record for this book is available from the British Library.

ISBN 1 85793 993 X

10 9 8 7 6 5 4 3 2 1

Printed in the United States of America

This book may be ordered by post from the publisher. Please contact the Marketing Department. But try your bookshop first.

Back Cover: Colourful Sesame Chicken and Snow Peas (Mange-Touts) in Apricot Sauce (recipe on page 140) is the main dish in a dinner (menu on page 129) that also includes a salad, pasta and cheesecake, yet contains just 675 calories and only 8 per-cent calories from fat.

Above Right: Treat someone special to a beautiful breakfast of Very Berry Waffles (recipe on page 67) that is high in fibre and get their day off to a healthy start.

Produced by Weldon Owen, Inc.
814 Montgomery Street
San Francisco, California 94133

Separations by Colourscan, Singapore

Printed by R.R. Donnelley
Willard, Ohio

Measurements listed in the nutritional analysis have been rounded off. Unless otherwise stated, the recipes were designed for medium-sized fruits and vegetables.

*This book is dedicated with love to people who,
like myself, want to know how to cook healthy meals that
are easy to prepare, delicious to eat and good for you.*
– Jane Fonda

Contents

Healthy Living

Enjoying Healthy Living

Cooking for healthy living means planning meals that make use of fresh foods, which are prepared to retain their nutrients and maximize their flavours. It means savouring seasonal produce and experiencing nature's broad palette of colours and flavours. It means enjoying delicious, satisfying meals with attention and deliberation and not rushing absent-mindedly through to the end. It means drinking water to lubricate your whole body. And, when combined with exercise, it means establishing and maintaining a metabolism that will let you eat more and weigh less.

Following these principles, you'll never have to diet and you'll never feel deprived. You'll eat wonderfully satisfying meals and you'll be in control of your weight. And you'll feel, act and look more healthy than ever before. In this introduction, I will share with you the nutritional principles and lifestyle habits that have made a profound difference in the quality and health of my life.

These introductory sections are intended to explain the sound nutritional principles behind the recipes and menus in this book. The recipes and menus have been developed in close collaboration with me by nutrition and cooking expert Robin Vitetta and a team of consultants to reflect my personal approach to healthy cooking and eating and to help you effortlessly adopt those principles.

First, however, I'd like to tell you about the paths in my life that have led me towards a greater awareness of what it means to eat healthily. I hope you'll find some parallels in your own experiences and take heart from the fact that, whatever your past, you *can* change the way you cook and eat, starting today.

It seems that whenever I read a good cookery book, it describes how the author grew up in a family that loved to cook, learned the basics by hanging round the kitchen at his or her father's or mother's elbow, and ever since then has enjoyed a lifelong passion for cooking. None of these things were particularly true for me. When I was growing up, we always had someone who cooked for us, and the kitchen was never a very welcoming place.

One thing from my childhood has had a lasting influence on my health, and that is eating fresh, seasonal produce. My father, Henry Fonda, a midwesterner by birth and by nature, was an avid gardener. As far back as I can remember, he enjoyed growing his own vegetables and fruit.

Until I was 10, we lived on a sort of farm in the foothills of the Santa Monica Mountains overlooking the Pacific Ocean. It was World War II, food was rationed and growing a Victory Garden was seen as an act of patriotism. At least to my young eyes, however,

Ours was more than just a garden. We had acres of vegetables and fruit trees and an enormous rabbit and chicken coop with individual pens for the laying hens, where their eggs would roll down into a trough to be gathered, still warm. To this day, I harbour a special fondness for fresh soft-boiled eggs.

It was on this farm, when he was not serving on a Navy destroyer in the Pacific, that my father taught me and my brother, Peter, about composting and how chicken droppings made the best fertilizer. I'm still proud that I can recognize rhubarb, asparagus and a host of other vegetables as their greenery first sprouts from the earth.

Towards the end of my father's life, he lived in the up-market Los Angeles enclave of Bel-Air. There he transformed a portion of his manicured property into vegetable gardens that followed the French intensive method of raised beds, better suited to a smaller area. He grew many fruit trees and raised bees for their honey. He even built a sizable chicken coop where the roosters' crowing gave proof that, though he was now famous and was living fancier, Henry Fonda was still a product of the Great Plains, a farmer at heart, willing to press his luck with local codes that forbade livestock.

My father's love of gardening taught me to appreciate freshly grown produce and to pass this appreciation, as if by osmosis, on to my children. My daughter Vanessa, in particular, follows in her grandfather's steps, avidly tending vegetables in a tiny plot behind her home in Washington, D.C.

Though I had little childhood experience in the kitchen, for better or worse

How to Use This Book

COOKING FOR HEALTHY LIVING has been created and structured to make it as easy as possible for you to incorporate principles of healthy cooking and eating into your life. The following features work together to make that goal attainable:

✳ **Introduction.** Please read over pages 8–29 for a comprehensive yet easy-to-follow discussion of healthy cooking and eating, the basic principles of nutrition, meal and menu planning, shopping tips, weight loss and exercise.

✳ **Suggested Menus.** Each of the three chapters on breakfast (page 30), lunch (page 78) and dinner (page 126) begins with 21 menus for complete, healthy meals. Please use these to help you plan your next day, week or month of healthy eating. Following each chapter's Suggested Menus are the featured recipes, accompanied by a beautiful photograph of the finished dish. The last chapter, Completing the Meal (page 174), presents the recipes that round out the menus — the drinks, side dishes, dressings and desserts — plus basic recipes and healthy cooking techniques referred to throughout the book. To help in your planning, each recipe includes preparation and cooking times, along with tips on substitutions, preparation techniques and storage information. The ingredients lists and cooking methods are simple and to the point, written so that even the beginner cook can make the dish perfectly the very first time.

✳ **Nutritional Analyses.** Each menu and individual recipe includes a nutritional analysis to assist you in planning your personal healthy-eating goals.

Example of a breakfast menu ———

Poached Fruit with Cinnamon Yogurt Topping
page 36

Where the recipe is located ———

Almond Biscotti
page 215

Example of a recipe for completing the meal ———

Skinny Café Mocha
page 179

Nutritional analysis for the menu ———

Nutritional Analysis per Serving: Calories 363 (Kilojoules 1,540); Total fat 5g; Saturated fat 1g; Protein 11g; Cholesterol 30mg; Carbohydrates 74g; Sodium 227mg; Dietary fibre 3g; Calories from fat 12%

I've cooked a lot since the time, at age 24, I moved to France and married film director Roger Vadim, father of my gardener-daughter. I became a cookery book aficionada, reading everything from *The Alice B. Toklas Cookbook* to Escoffier's classic *Le Guide Culinaire*.

In early 1960s pre-supermarket France, shopping for groceries in my halting French, I must have seemed like a blind woman on a scavenger hunt. Vegetables were found only in the vegetable market, fish in the fish market, bread in the *boulangerie*. I remember the consequences of my first sortie to shop for a steak dinner. About five minutes into the meal, Vadim looked up and asked where I'd bought the meat.

"At the butcher," I said.

"Was there a horse's head over the door?"

In a flash, I realized what I'd done. Horse meat! I had cooked my favourite animal!

Though I never made that mistake again, I was a pretty adventuresome cook. The first time Vadim's ex-wife came over for dinner, I was really nervous. And why not? After all, she was Brigitte Bardot. I cooked *boudin noir,* "blood sausage". Maybe I was sending Brigitte a subliminal message. Neither of them suspected that I'd never seen a blood sausage in my life, much less cooked or eaten one.

My poor daughter took the brunt of my early efforts at healthy cooking. I so very much wanted to make sure she started her little life with the best possible nutrition. My bible at the time was health-food guru Adele Davis's *Let's Eat Right to Keep Fit.* When I weaned my daughter at four months, I put her on the formula Davis recommended: goat's milk, cranberry juice concentrate, a little yeast and *desiccated baby veal liver.* Needless to say, I had to make the hole in the nipple larger. When I eventually told a doctor what I had been feeding her and asked why she kept throwing up, he just stared at me in disbelief.

My father, Henry Fonda, shown here in a 1948 magazine photo, rides a tractor that was the pride and joy of his garden. He received the tractor for appearing on a Ford radio programme. Known among his neighbours as the Compost King, he grew apples, oranges, berries and all the vegetables for our family's table.

My most memorable failure came at my daughter's third birthday party. I had followed a recipe for a wholewheat birthday cake. As I walked from the kitchen carrying the cake with its candles aglow, I slipped. The cake shattered like a brick on the floor, necessitating a scramble to the bakery for the traditional, disgustingly gooey, undeniably delicious cake.

Since those Paris days, I've come a long way in my approach to healthy cooking and eating. Three-and-a-half decades of dealing with the demands put on a professional actress to look good in a close-up after 15 hours on a soundstage have taught me sensible ways to eat meals that provide energy and vitality, are satisfying and tasty, and won't put on weight.

When I entered the health and fitness business in the late 1970s, I began working with dieticians, doctors and sports physicians to learn the best ways to achieve maximum health through diet and exercise. As a mother, I learned the importance of serving well-balanced meals made up of a wide variety of fresh,

Karen Averitt (left) and I confer with Recipe Writer Robin Vitetta (right) in my Montana kitchen. Karen and I have worked together since the early 1980s. Several of her best recipes appear among the menus Robin developed for this book.

whole (non-processed) foods, cooked in ways that best retain their natural nutrients.

These days, I must admit, my fondness for really good food far exceeds my ability to cook it. Even if that weren't the case, there's not much time for me to do the cooking, since we entertain a lot and I, my husband, Ted Turner, and our frequent guests are usually outdoors right up until mealtime.

For that reason, the recipes in this book reflect not what I myself cook, but rather how I like to eat. I do, however, plan all our menus, and I am exceedingly fortunate to employ three talented people – in three different parts of the country where, depending on the season, we spend our non-working time – who cook for us, following my dietary guidelines. These expert cooks have skilfully learned to adapt their regional styles to suit our desire for healthy meals.

In particular, I want to mention Karen Averitt, my longtime friend and associate who cooks for us when we are in Montana. When I ran a health spa she managed the operation, prepared the meals and taught spa cooking. When Ted and I married, Karen and her musician-husband, Jim Averitt, moved to our ranch in Montana. Karen has learned to adjust her rather stringent spa menus to please my husband's Southern palate while keeping them healthy. She has developed a variety of wonderful low-fat ways to cook the fish, wildfowl and game that we catch, and the delicious free-range bison that we raise.

I have finally learned that healthy food doesn't have to be boring or strange. It can be so delicious that your family and friends won't even suspect that you're feeding them responsibly.

In this book, I want to teach you what I've learned about how to eat to maximize your health and energy; how to avoid over-eating; and, for those interested in losing weight, how eating and exercise, like love and marriage, go together. You *can* make healthy eating and healthy living part and parcel of your life every day – morning, noon and night.

Understanding Wellness

"We need networks of bike paths and jogging trails, neighbourhoods that are designed for walking, safe streets that kids can play in, schools that encourage children to develop a lifelong love of physical activity, restaurant menus that list calories, and fun-filled activities that make young people not want to watch television."
— Michael F. Jacobson, Ph.D.
Executive Director, Center for Science in the Public Interest

Wellness has become a catchword in recent years for those of us interested in healthy living. Yet the concept isn't all that easy to grasp. That's because wellness isn't just the absence of illness and it isn't something you can achieve with a quick medical fix.

Wellness is a way of life. It takes into account the totality of your being: body, mind and spirit, both individually and in relation to each other. To achieve deep, true wellness, all three must be nourished.

This book seeks to help nourish the body. In doing so, it will also affect the mind and the spirit. And while you're thinking about life changes, why not also see what you can do in your community to bring about the changes Michael Jacobson envisions in the quote above, thus improving your own wellness and that of the people around you?

The Way We Eat

Human beings have many complex reasons for eating. It offers us a comforting social ritual, drowns our sorrows, fills the empty places in our heart or brings us pleasure.

Few of us give much thought to whether the sum of what we eat on any given day does what food is supposed to do: nourish us, providing the fuel and the building blocks our bodies need.

Whatever their function, each of the microscopic cells in our bodies is like a miniature factory. To do a good job, they require the best raw materials. Too often, these cells are plagued by pollutants – specifically substances called free radicals, which result from normal metabolic processes as well as from air pollution, cigarette smoke (ours or someone else's) and ozone. Free radicals cause cell damage and are a key factor in the aging process. Anti-oxidants – including vitamins C and E, beta-carotene and the mineral selenium – reduce the damaging effects. A healthy diet includes ample amounts of foods containing anti-oxidants.

The foods most of us eat on a daily basis, however, sorely lack these and other vital substances in sufficient quantities to keep our bodies working well. Instead, they include an excess of nutrients that slow us down and even damage us. Consider that 62 per-cent of the calories we put into our mouths comes from sugar, animal fats and alcohol, which have no fibre and little nutritive value. I like to refer to this as the Standard American Diet, with the all-too-fitting acronym SAD (see sidebar, page 14). The SAD diet accelerates the aging process by depriving our cells of the nutrients they need to regenerate and fight off the many environmental factors that bombard us daily.

Potentially Preventable Causes of Death in the United States

The SAD diet of processed-sugar breakfasts, fast-food lunches and dinners heavy on red meat is a recipe for disaster. As you can see in this chart, from the "Journal of the American Medical Association," the Standard American Diet is our biggest killer, with 300,000-plus deaths a year attributable to diet and lack of exercise.

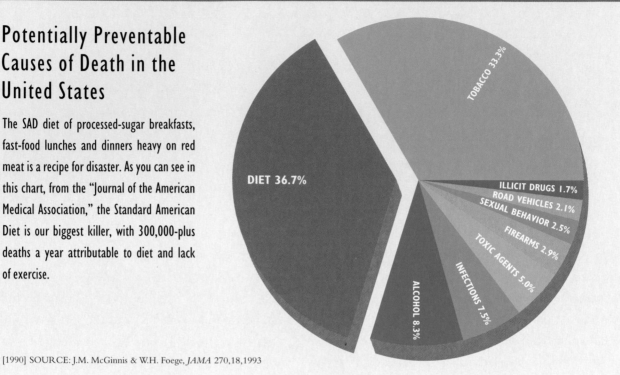

DIET 36.7%
TOBACCO 33.3%
ILLICIT DRUGS 1.7%
ROAD VEHICLES 2.1%
SEXUAL BEHAVIOR 2.5%
FIREARMS 2.9%
TOXIC AGENTS 5.0%
INFECTIONS 7.5%
ALCOHOL 8.3%

[1990] SOURCE: J.M. McGinnis & W.H. Foege, *JAMA* 270,18,1993

It's little wonder Americans tend to be unhealthy. Even the $35 billion fitness industry can't compete with this nation's always convenient 150,000 fast-food outlets and 4 million food vending machines, as well as a popular culture that promotes eating and lethargy over health and exercise. Too many of our children recognize sugary breakfast cereals more readily than fresh produce. We ride instead of walk, take elevators instead of stairs. We sit in front of our TVs an average of four hours a day – a figure even higher for the average teenager.

With medical costs ever rising and with so many things assaulting us that are beyond our immediate control, doesn't it make sense to take charge of the things we *can*? Wellness *can* begin at home – in what we cook and eat. It isn't difficult.

In fact, committing to a healthier way of eating can be easy and painless – and I'd like to show you how. It begins with learning a little bit more about the nutritional values of foods and how our bodies use them. With this knowledge, you can more easily plan your meals – a particularly important step for those seeking to lose weight and a step most often over-looked. Plan in hand, you can shop more sensibly. Using easy methods that most of us already know, you can cook food to maximize its taste and texture and preserve its nutritional value without adding calories or fat. Then, with the help of some simple strategies for modifying your behaviour, you can actually eat that food in a different way that will bring you more pleasure, a greater sense of satisfaction and even, should you require it, weight loss.

Knowing Nutritional Basics

Here are the basic nutritional terms you'll need to understand when planning, shopping for, cooking and eating healthy meals: calories, protein, fat, saturated fat, cholesterol, carbohydrates, fibre and sodium. They form the basis for the nutritional analysis that accompanies every menu and recipe in this book. Use them as a guide in the long-term planning process.

Calories

For nutritional purposes, calories measure the amount of energy any given ingredient or finished recipe will provide you. We need a specific number of calories daily from food, depending on our size, weight, activity level and resting metabolism – the amount of energy a body must have simply to function. Eat more calories than you burn and you gain weight; eat fewer calories than you burn and you lose weight. One calorie is equal to 4.2 kilojoules – a term used instead of calories in some countries.

Protein

Present in seafood, poultry, meats, dairy products, pulses and grains, protein builds and repairs tissues and performs other essential functions. One gram yields about 4 calories (17 kilojoules) of energy, and a healthy diet will derive about 15 per-cent of daily calories from protein – the equivalent of about 185 grams (6 ounces) of seafood, poultry or meat. However, many people eat twice as much protein as they need; often, with it comes extra fat.

Fat

Everybody needs to eat some fat. It supplies us with fatty acids – essential substances that help move fat-soluble vitamins throughout our bodies – and also helps form and maintain the body fat we need for cushioning and insulation, stored energy, supple skin, healthy hair and some hormonal functions. One gram of fat yields 9 calories (38 kilojoules) of energy.

The trouble is, most of us eat far more fat than our bodies need, and too much of it in the form of saturated fat, instead of unsaturated fats that can decrease the overall level of blood cholesterol.

For the recipes in this book, I have aimed for an average of 25 per-cent of daily calories from fat; if you want to facilitate weight loss, choose those recipes with an even lower percentage.

You'll see that a few of the recipes derive more than 25 per-cent of their calories from fat. This doesn't mean you should avoid them. Rather, such recipes as Eggs Benedict (page 76) and Greek Salad (page 112) let you enjoy reduced-fat versions of high-fat dishes. As shown in the Suggested Menus in which such recipes are included, combine them with dishes that yield a lower overall fat content and choose low-fat recipes for your remaining meals that day.

Saturated Fat

No more than one-third of the day's total fat calories should come from saturated fat, present in animal proteins and in vegetable fats like palm and coconut oils. Saturated fat from animal proteins contains cholesterol, and all saturated fats increase the production of cholesterol by the liver – thereby raising total blood cholesterol levels.

Cholesterol

We could not live without cholesterol, which helps build hormones, cell membranes and nerve fibre sheaths. But our livers produce all we need.

When we eat too much saturated fat and animal protein and don't exercise enough, excessive cholesterol is deposited on arterial walls. The result: high blood pressure, stroke and heart disease. Experts agree that we should eat no more than 300 milligrams of dietary cholesterol a day.

Carbohydrates

Carbohydrates are the main source of energy in a healthy diet and should provide about 55 per-cent or more of our daily calories. They are classed into two categories: simple carbohydrates (sugars) and complex carbohydrates (starches). Like protein, one gram of carbohydrate yields about 4 calories (17 kilojoules).

When carbohydrates are digested, they become glucose – blood sugar. Glucose provides energy for the brain, the nervous system and the muscles, and must be available for a muscle cell to burn fat.

Simple carbohydrates are rapidly converted to glucose and absorbed into the bloodstream. In excess, they give an immediate energy burst, often swiftly followed by a precipitous drop. These so-called empty calories lack any other nutrients. Yet, avoiding them can be difficult, considering that 70 per-cent of the sugar in the average person's daily regimen is hidden in soft drinks, canned fruit, processed meat and commercial cereals. No more than 10 per-cent of total daily carbohydrate calories should come from sugars.

Foods high in complex carbohydrates – whole grains, pastas, cereals, breads, vegetables, pulses – are the fundamental wellness foods. Slowly digested, they supply steady energy, are chock-full of vitamins and minerals and are your best source of fibre.

Fibre

The body can't digest or absorb fibre, the residue from plant foods. Soluble fibre, which dissolves in water, slows down the digestion of carbohydrates, enabling their glucose to enter the bloodstream more slowly and yielding sustained energy. Soluble fibre also helps flush out cholesterol and toxins. It is abundant in oat bran, pulses and citrus fruits.

Insoluble fibre remains intact, absorbing water, expanding in the stomach and helping to pass food more quickly through the digestive tract while also sweeping out toxins. Insoluble fibre is found in whole grains, lentils, wheat bran, celery and beets.

Both kinds of fibre promote healthy, regular elimination. Experts recommend eating 18 grams a day.

Sodium

Sodium is widely misunderstood. Some of the mineral is needed by our bodies to help maintain proper levels of water, acids and bases and to regulate hormonal functions. However, we consume far too much of it. This comes not only through the salt we sprinkle on our food – about 2,200 milligrams per teaspoon – but also through its natural occurrence in many ingredients and its high levels in processed and snack foods. Most bodies eliminate excess sodium naturally; others tend to retain it. High levels of sodium lead to water retention, which can lead to high blood pressure. Drinking ample water daily helps flush out sodium. Experts recommend we eat between 1,100 and 3,300 milligrams of sodium a day.

The Food Pyramid

To help Americans easily understand the elements of a healthy daily diet, the United States Department of Agriculture and the United States Department of Health and Human Services jointly developed the Food Guide Pyramid, introduced in 1991. It clearly illustrates what proportion of a daily diet should be made up of each basic food group.

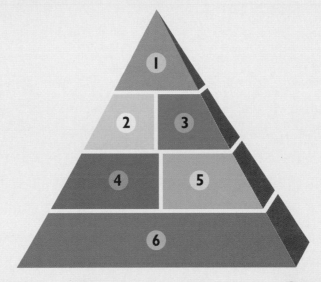

6 Breads, Cereals, Rice and Pasta: 6–11 servings

These abundant sources of complex carbohydrates, fibre and minerals provide most daily calories. One serving: 1 slice bread; 90 g (3 oz) cooked cereal, rice or pasta; 30 g (1 oz) ready-to-eat cereal; 1 pancake.

5 Vegetables: 3–5 servings

Excellent sources of vitamins, minerals and fibre, vegetables are also low in fat. One serving: 60 g (2 oz) raw leafy vegetables; 90 g (3 oz) cooked or chopped raw vegetables; 185 ml (6 fl oz) vegetable juice.

4 Fruits: 2–4 servings

Fruits are excellent sources of vitamins A and C, folic acid and potassium; eaten whole, they are also high in fibre. One serving: 1 medium apple, banana or orange; 90 g (3 oz) chopped, cooked or canned fruit; 45 g (1½ oz) dried fruit; 185 ml (6 fl oz) fruit juice.

3 Dairy Products: 2–3 servings

Milk, yogurt and cheese are good sources of protein, vitamins and minerals and are the best sources of calcium. One serving: 250 ml (8 fl oz) milk; 250 g (8 oz) yogurt; 45 g (1½ oz) cheese; 500 g (1 lb) cottage cheese.

2 Proteins: 2–3 servings

Meat, poultry, fish, beans, eggs and nuts provide protein, B vitamins, iron and zinc. For the lowest fat, choose lean meats, skinless poultry, seafood, beans and lentils. One serving: 60–90g (2–3 oz) cooked seafood, skinless poultry or lean meat; 105 g (3½ oz) cooked dried beans; 1 egg.

1 Fats, Oils and Sweets: use sparingly

It is difficult to avoid some fats and sugars present naturally in foods. You can avoid consuming candy, cooking fats and foods processed with added sugar.

Planning Meals

With the knowledge of how basic nutrients make up a healthy daily diet and the serving numbers recommended on the Food Pyramid (see page 17), you can begin to plan your meals. Planning serves several useful purposes.

First, it lets you map out precisely what you will eat, ensuring a healthy balance of foods. Planning also provides you with a good shopping list, compiled from the ingredient lists of the recipes you plan to make. Not only will that list make shopping more convenient and economical, but it will guard against impulse buys of less healthy foods. If you are trying to lose weight, planning will help you reinforce your self-discipline.

Planning also helps you ensure another important aspect of healthy eating: variety. None of us can possibly manage to eat every single nutrient we need every single day. What is more important is to eat a varied diet that, over several days or a week, provides the full range of vitamins and minerals along with the more basic nutrients. Planning is the key to building variety into our diets.

Recognizing the importance of planning, 21 Suggested Menus lead off each of the next three chapters in this book to help you plan your meals for several weeks.

Breakfast

Breakfast is the perfect start to a day of healthy eating. Never skip it. If you do, or if you eat an inadequate breakfast, by late morning your energy will start to flag, and there's a good chance, unless you've thought to bring along a healthy snack, you'll try to pick yourself up with more coffee or a sugary treat.

A good breakfast featuring sufficient complex carbohydrates will digest slowly, gradually raising your blood sugar level and supplying steady energy. You should also include a small amount of protein, most conveniently in the form of milk or yogurt. This also supplies essential calcium and additional carbohydrate energy from milk sugar, or lactose. Those of us who have trouble digesting lactose can substitute soy milk.

Because eating for healthy living doesn't mean sacrificing all of your pleasures and giving up every habit, we've included coffee and tea on the Suggested Breakfast Menus (beginning on page 32). Whether or not they contain caffeine is your choice. A small glass of fruit juice, also listed with most breakfasts, is a good way to obtain a fruit serving.

Right: A wedge of Green Pepper-Corn Frittata, half an English muffin and a Strawberry Banana Shake make up a well-planned breakfast (menu on page 35) that fulfills grain, protein, vegetable and fruit servings in only 383 calories for the complete meal.

Snacks as Good Food

Many nutritionists sing the praises of dividing up the traditional three meals into several smaller meals eaten throughout the day. That isn't very practical for most people. But it is a good idea to have small portions of easy, healthy between-meal snacks on hand to stave off hunger, provide extra energy and help you avoid overeating later.

Here are some suggestions:

✳ Have a bowl of washed seasonal fruit always available on your counter or table.

✳ Prepare carrot and celery sticks, raw cabbage and chicory and have them ready to eat in the refrigerator.

✳ Pop air-popped popcorn.

✳ Carry salt-free rice cakes for coffee breaks.

✳ Cook your own baked tortilla chips (recipe on page 115) instead of buying salty commercial ones.

✳ Bake an extra potato for a snack (good-quality potatoes are delicious plain at room temperature).

✳ Drink a Smoothie (recipe on page 176) when you feel you must have something sweet.

✳ Substitute virtually no fat yogurt or Raspberry Sherbet (recipe on page 224) for ice cream snacks.

✳ Drink a glass of water when you feel hungry.

Lunch

Lunch is the best time to fill your daily protein requirements, accompanied by a variety of complex carbohydrates. Soup makes an especially satisfying lunch that meets your protein and carbohydrate needs while being lower in calories than solid foods – provided the soup has been de-fatted and made without cream or butter. Properly seasoned with herbs or spices, it won't be high in sodium, either. Because soup is usually hot, we tend to eat it more slowly than solid foods and wind up feeling full with a small portion.

If you work away from your home and don't have access to a cafeteria or restaurant that offers a good salad bar and other healthy selections, try brown-bagging it. Many of the lunch menus in this book pack easily. You'll need a wide-mouthed vacuum bottle for soup, cooked proteins, pasta or grains; an airtight container for salads or sandwich fillings; and a smaller container for dressing. Pack bread separately, building your sandwich at the last minute so it won't get soggy. Brown-bagging should save you time, too, providing a few extra minutes to take a midday walk or to have a workout at a nearby gym!

As you can see from the menus in this book, I don't favour fruit salad as the lunch main course. Such a concentration of sugars, even though they are natural ones, will give you quick energy but leave you drooping by mid-afternoon. If you are eating out and fruit salad is the only healthy option on the menu, have it with some protein – such as low-fat cottage cheese or yogurt – and some complex carbohydrates for more sustained energy.

However, because people often have trouble including enough fruit in their diets, especially in winter, a piece of fruit and fruit juice are listed with most of the Suggested Lunch Menus (beginning on page 80) You may want to save the fruit for an afternoon snack. Drinking fruit juice with lunch, as with breakfast, is a good way to increase your fruit intake. Several of the menus suggest mixing fruit juice with seltzer water. This refreshing combination provides the bubbles of a soda without the caffeine.

Dinner

Although you can't always control when you eat at night, it's best not to eat dinner too late. In a well-publicized study, a group of people ate one 2,000-calorie (8,400-kilojoule) meal a day as either breakfast, lunch or dinner. Those who ate breakfast lost weight, those who ate lunch maintained their weight, and those who ate dinner gained weight.

Dinner should emphasize complex carbohydrates, with proteins used in small portions – almost like a garnish. Because they are bulky and take longer to digest, complex carbohydrates leave you feeling more satisfied – and less likely to snack later. Some researchers also think that they trigger the release in the brain of serotonin, a chemical that, among other functions, has a soothing effect, promoting better sleep. (It is interesting to note that the much-touted prescription drug Prozac helps the brain maintain levels of that same chemical.)

The Suggested Dinner Menus (beginning on page 128) all include dessert. Desserts do not have to be sinful to be delicious. Many of the desserts in this book are healthier versions of traditional sweets and others feature fruit as a main ingredient. While you may not want dessert every evening, when you do, these suggestions provide new options for a healthy ending to a meal.

No drinks are listed with the dinner menus and water is shown in the accompanying photographs.

The Importance of Water

We need to drink eight 250 ml (8 fl oz) glasses of water — not just liquids but pure water — every day. Too few of us do, and we take water so much for granted that we often fail to recognize the signs that we need it. We might feel sluggish or hungry when, in fact, we are dehydrated.

I cannot stress to you what a difference it can make to the way you feel to remain hydrated throughout the day.

Following my husband's example, at the beginning of 1994 I made a New Year's resolution to drink all the water I really needed. I carry with me a tall plastic bottle and make a point of drinking from it regularly over the course of the day, so that by bedtime it is empty. Every morning I refill the same bottle from a 5- or 10-gallon bottle of water.

I now feel less hungry throughout the day, especially when I drink a glass or two before a meal. My skin and hair are less dry. And I can see that water has a natural diuretic effect, largely eliminating fluid retention and bloating.

I find that it's easier to keep my water always with me if I carry my bottle in a holder with a shoulder strap. You'll find these in outdoor and camping suppliers.

There are many other strategies you can use. Have a glass each morning in place of that second cup of coffee. Substitute it for an afternoon soda, adding a slice of citrus fruit. In your car, take a sip at every red light.

There are many strategies, once you think of water as liquid breath. Keep it flowing through you, moistening and cleansing your body.

Shopping Wisely

I remember once telling Katharine Hepburn how good her cooking was. She replied, in her inimitable voice, "It's because I know how to shop!"

Experienced cooks firmly believe that knowing how to shop is essential to cooking tasty meals. A wise shopper can pick the best-quality ingredients, with the best taste, texture and nutritive value — at the best cost. Here are my tips:

✶ **Buy locally produced food.** That sounds like a simple statement, but there's a complex truth behind it best expressed in the book *Eight Simple Steps to the New Green Diet* by Mothers & Others for a Livable Planet: "The average mouthful of food travels 1,200 miles from farm to factory to warehouse to supermarket to our plates. In comparison, food available from local farms is almost always fresher, tastier, and closer to ripeness. . . . And, because it isn't being shipped long distances, local food is less likely to have been treated with post-harvest pesticides."

✶ **Develop sources.** Learn where you can buy the best quality and selection of fresh herbs, spices, dried beans and peas, rice, whole-grain cereals and breads.

✶ **Seek out organic products.** Organic foods are better for us and the environment. Organic fruits and vegetables are grown without pesticides or chemical fertilizers. Organic meats and poultry are raised without antibiotics or growth hormones.

Ask around for the best organic food market near you. Support organically grown foods and the people who produce and sell them so there will be a bigger demand, which will result in higher production and lower prices. If buying organic is not an option for you, don't feel any guilt about disregarding this tip. Just be very sure to wash produce well, scrubbing the fruits and vegetables you'll be eating, peels and all, to remove any traces of chemicals.

✶ **Seek out seasonal produce.** Again, I want to quote *Eight Simple Steps to the New Green Diet*: "Out-of-season produce is extravagant, because it is so amazingly energy-intensive. It costs about 435 calories [1,830 kilojoules] to fly one five-calorie [21-kilojoule] strawberry from California to New York. Out-of-season produce is also more likely to have been imported, possibly from a country with less stringent pesticide regulations than the U.S. Eating frozen fruits and vegetables, especially from local producers, is your very best option during the winter months. Frozen foods retain much of their nutritional content, in addition to cutting energy costs."

✶ **Patronize a local butcher.** If you cannot find a source for naturally raised meat or poultry, at least find a market where you can buy your meat fresh. Ask the butcher to cut it to order, and request that all excess fat be trimmed away.

✶ **Consider game.** Though I am not a vegetarian, I eat meat only in small portions, and for the most part, my family gets animal protein from elk, deer, bison and game birds. Game has far less fat and no chemical additives. Bison, for example, is lower in fat and cholesterol than chicken or turkey.

When You Must Substitute

The numbers below demonstrate why low-fat products are so helpful in creating healthy meals. When you must substitute other products, be sure to read product labels and adjust your nutritional analysis accordingly.

	CALORIES	TOTAL FAT (g)	SATURATED FAT (g)	CHOLESTEROL (mg)	SODIUM (mg)	CALORIES FROM FAT
per 100 ml:						
Whole Milk	68	4.0 g	2.5 g	14 mg	57 mg	5%
Semi-skimmed Milk	49	1.7 g	1 g	7 mg	57 mg	3%
Skimmed Milk	34	0.1 g	0.06 g	2 mg	57 mg	3%
per 100 g:						
Low-fat Plain Yogurt	56	0.8 g	0.5 g	4 mg	83 mg	13%
Very Low-fat Plain Yogurt	41	0.2 g	0.1 g	1 mg	73 mg	4%
Unsalted Butter	737	82.7 g	54 g	230 mg	11 mg	100%
Salted Polyunsaturated Margarine	739	81.6 g	25 g	9 mg	800 mg	99%

✳ **Shop along the supermarket's walls.** Concentrate on fresh produce and on low-fat dairy products, seafood, poultry and meats – all products commonly displayed along the walls. Go for a variety of produce colours, since each one offers different nutritional value. Most important are dark greens such as broccoli and cabbage, reds such as peppers and tomatoes, and yellows and oranges like cantaloupes, carrots and winter squashes.

✳ **Buy fresh produce at frequent intervals.** Try not to buy too much fresh fruit and vegetables at any one time. They begin to lose half their vitamin C after two or three days in the refrigerator, and even more quickly at room temperature.

✳ **Buy any frozen foods last.** To keep these in the best condition, put them in your cart just before you go to the check-out.

✳ **Avoid empty calories.** Shop with an eye towards getting the most nutritive bang for your buck and your calories. This means avoiding processed foods, which usually cost more and are far higher in fat, sugar and salt than fresh foods.

✳ **Make a list.** Have a list to help you avoid impulse buying, especially when you get in the aisles where soft drinks, sweets and processed foods are stocked.

✳ **Learn to read labels.** Packaged products now carry labels that give all the pertinent information on nutrition content. A careful look at the ingredients list of a packaged product will also tip you off to the presence of monosodium glutamate, preservatives and other chemical additives.

✳ **Don't shop when hungry.** You'll make a wiser purchase, and spend less, if you shop on a full stomach. Drink some water before entering the market. If you still feel hungry, pick up a banana, a small pack of brown rice cakes or some other healthy snack and eat it while you shop. (Needless to say, save the peel or wrapper and tell the cashier to ring it up.)

Eating to Lose Weight

Like many women, I have not always had a healthy relationship with food. Perhaps that is why, today, I feel such sweet pleasure at being able to eat normally, healthily and without anxiety. I can do this because I have studied the effects different foods have on the body, I have learned the physiology of weight gain, and I have discovered, sometimes through hard experience, just how counter-productive dieting is. I've also worked on developing positive mental health.

There was a time not so long ago when the phrase "eating to lose weight" would have seemed an oxymoron. Losing weight meant not eating. In those days, I would starve myself, sometimes eating fewer than 500 calories a day and thinking even that was too much. I remember saying to anyone who commented on my radically restricted eating habits, "If I even eat an apple, I will put on weight."

I was right. My body was so starved that it burned muscle tissue to get the energy it needed. Because of the loss of muscle tissue, I had a very low metabolism. Anything I ate would be hoarded by my body as fat.

Today, I eat normal amounts of a wide variety of foods. Had I known sooner what I know now about how to avoid counter-productive dieting, how much easier and healthier my life would have been.

Consider the word *diet*. It derives from the Greek *diaita,* meaning "manner of living". That's what a weight-loss programme should be: not some on-again off-again, feast-and-famine seesaw but a permanent, balanced, sustainable, metabolism-raising way of life.

Why Humans Store Fat

The roots of many people's weight problems may be found in evolution. Ten thousand years ago, humans lived as hunter-gatherers, moving with the seasons, searching constantly for adequate food supplies. The foods most reliably available were carbohydrate-rich vegetables and fruits. As a result, the human body did not need to develop a capacity for storing within itself large amounts of carbohydrates.

Meat was far more difficult to obtain. It would be eaten immediately, since meat was harder to store. Long periods of time might go by, especially during winter, when there would be no available fat, a crucial source of energy. We adapted by developing the ability to store fat within our bodies.

Today, our bodies still have a limited capacity for storing carbohydrates and an unlimited capacity for storing fat. We are sedentary, eating diets high in fats and sugars. No wonder some 26 per-cent of Americans are clinically obese.

Healthy Eating Out

Restaurants

Good restaurants are accustomed to special requests and are happy to comply.

✳ **Order small, healthy portions.** Ask for a salad or soup (made without cream or butter) as your starter. Then order another starter as your main course.

✳ **Ask for salad dressing on the side.** If you need the taste of dressing, dip your fork before you spear some lettuce.

✳ **Make special requests.** Don't feel self-conscious about asking for food cooked without butter, cream, salt and MSG.

✳ **Have a main course strategy.** Choose main courses that are broiled, steamed, roasted, poached or grilled. Ask for sauces on the side. Split one main course with a companion or eat half and take the rest home for another meal.

✳ **Don't make a big deal about food preferences.** It's always a drag when someone goes on about his or her diet. Quietly and gracefully relay your requests to the waiter.

Air Travel

It is perfectly possible today to eat healthy food on an airplane.

✳ **Phone ahead.** Most airlines offer healthier options such as low-fat, low-calorie seafood, fruit and vegetarian meals. Call at least 6 and usually 24 hours ahead.

✳ **Pack your own meal.** With the help of airtight, resealable bags and containers, ice packs and lightweight insulated carriers, pack a delicious, healthy carry-on meal.

✳ **Eat moderately, drink lavishly.** Eat as little as possible without being hungry and drink a lot of water. At least one glass every hour helps offset the dehydration caused by cabin pressurization and will minimize jet lag. Avoid alcohol.

Fast Food

Here's how you can make the best of fast-food restaurants.

✳ **Take the fresh approach.** Whenever possible, stick to salad bars, choosing only fresh vegetables and fruits.

✳ **Request nutrition details.** Most fast-food chains have flyers that provide nutritional analyses. Look them over.

✳ **Choose obvious low-fat options.** Select a grilled chicken sandwich. Ask for no sauce. Avoid fried foods.

✳ **Create your own pizza.** Order thin-crust pizza by the slice with vegetable toppings and without cheese. Fresh-baked crust topped with sauce and vegetables is delicious.

✳ **Have a high-fibre breakfast.** Stick to wholewheat toast or pancakes — without butter or syrup. Avoid egg sandwiches, bacon, sausage and croissants. Choose only low-fat muffins.

Automobile Travel

Here are some ways to break the habit of eating in your car.

✳ **Keep water handy.** If you feel hungry or tired, take a swig from a water bottle.

✳ **Lock temptations in the trunk.** Put the groceries in the boot, out of temptation's way.

Banquets and Parties

Help yourself with these strategies.

✳ **Special-order your food.** Call the restaurant, catering office or party planners at least 24 hours ahead and order a vegetable plate.

✳ **Don't linger around buffets.** Sip water and mingle!

✳ **Keep dessert away.** Put a coffee cup or glass right in front of you, so the waiter can't even set down a dessert plate.

Of course, a number of other factors also come into play, including genetics, low metabolism and simple lack of physical activity. It is clear that we have to take matters into our own hands, combining moderate exercise with sensible low-fat eating.

Why Not Dieting?

Scientists have come to believe in what is called the Set Point Theory, which asserts that within each of us is a sort of thermostat that kicks into action if our body suddenly loses too much fat, nitrogen and potassium, attempting to bring us back to our set point by increasing our appetite. It also causes the body to consume muscle tissue for the energy that should be coming from food, causing our metabolism to drop and diminishing our ability to burn the calories from the food we consume.

So what, then, does "eating to lose weight" mean? First of all, it means eating enough food to keep you from feeling hungry and deprived and your "thermostat" from kicking into fat-retaining mode. Then, to have energy and good health, we have to eat a wide variety of healthy foods, without eating more than our metabolism can "burn" as energy. In addition, we must try to maintain an appropriate amount of muscle mass to ensure a healthy metabolism.

Switching to a low-fat diet makes cutting calories a lot easier – particularly when you consider that a gram of fat has 9 calories (38 kilojoules), while a gram of protein or carbohydrate has just 4 calories (17 kilojoules). You can eat a greater volume of low-fat food without risking weight gain.

However, don't think that, just because something is "fat-free", we can eat all we want. Always bear in mind that *calories do count*, whether from fat or from fat-free foods. If we eat more calories than we burn, they will be stored as fat no matter what their source.

Strategies for Eating Less

✳ **Keep a food diary.** Write down everything to see how much you eat without being aware of it.

✳ **Measure portions.** Measure the food you eat until you have internalized what correct portions look like – and how you feel after eating them.

✳ **Drink water.** Have a large glass before every meal.

✳ **Serve food on smaller plates.** Smaller portions will appear proportionately bigger.

✳ **Eat slowly.** It takes our brains about 20 minutes from the time we start eating to register that hunger has been satisfied. Eat more slowly, and you'll consume less food in that time. Take small bites, chew each at least 20 times and pause between bites.

✳ **Don't let yourself get hungry.** Notice the times of day when your energy tends to flag and make sure you have a healthy, low-fat snack close at hand.

✳ **Do something else instead of eat.** When you feel the urge to eat and it's not mealtime, try to do something active like taking a brisk walk.

✳ **Don't eat when feeling anxious.** Learn ways to keep tension at bay. Relax and breathe deeply until the feeling passes. Yoga is a good way to handle tension and anxiety.

✳ **Be easy on yourself.** Everyone lapses from time to time. If you really crave a cheeseburger, have one. But then adjust what else you eat that day or the next. Don't let a little lapse turn into a relapse.

✳ **Remember: You're in control.** If you feel there is some vague authority figure saying, "You shouldn't eat this" and "You're bad if you do", you may react by over-eating to spite that voice. Instead, relax, breathe deeply and take back control.

✳ **Make meals pleasurable occasions.** Set a pretty table. Light candles. Play music with a slow tempo to set your eating pace. Talk. The more enjoyable a meal, the more slowly you will eat.

Eating and Exercise

I've said it before, but here it is once again: For sustainable weight loss, you must burn more calories than you consume. Nutritionists estimate that an average active woman can lose weight eating 1,200 to 1,300 calories (5,040 to 5,460 kilojoules) a day and maintain her weight eating 1,600 to 1,900 calories (6,720 to 7,980 kilojoules) a day; the average man can lose weight eating 1,700 to 1,800 calories (7,140 to 7,560 kilojoules) daily and maintain his weight eating 2,000 to 2,400 calories (8,400 to 10,080 kilojoules). To achieve or maintain your desired weight (assuming your idea of desired weight is reasonable), you should eat within those calorie amounts and establish a regular programme of physical activity.

Go for the Burn – the *Metabolic* Burn

By eating healthily and increasing the amount of exercise you do, you can raise your metabolism, reversing the vicious cycle of yo-yo dieting.

Think of your metabolism as, in part, the internal combustion that occurs in the cells of your body when digested fats, proteins and carbohydrates are "burned" to create energy, measured in calories. If we eat more calories than we burn, they will be stored as fat.

Sixty to 75 per-cent of the calories we burn each day are used to keep the body functioning while we are awake but resting. This is called our *resting metabolic rate* (RMR). As we exercise or just go about our lives, we use our muscles and thereby increase our output of energy above our RMR. Muscle is *active* tissue, and the more muscle we have, the higher our metabolism will be and the more calories we will burn.

Muscle is denser and more brick-like than spongy fat. That's why we can lose 1.5 kg (3 lb) of fat, gain 1.5 kg (3 lb) of muscle, not show any weight loss on the scale, but find our pants have become loose.

In short, the more lean muscle your body has, the higher your metabolic rate will be and the greater the number of calories you will burn just being alive.

It might interest you to know that middle-age spread is only partly due to the tendency to be less active as we age. The other reason is because we lose 3 to 5 per-cent of our muscle tissue each decade after age 30. This results in a slowing of our resting metabolic rate – unless we consciously work to increase our lean mass through exercise.

Train for Strength

You can increase your metabolism by building and maintaining your muscles. That doesn't mean you have to become bulked up like a weight lifter; instead, it just requires strengthening and toning your body through training with light weights. Although this can't reverse age-related loss of muscle tissue, it can definitely slow that loss and even restore some lost muscle tissue. It also will ensure that you maintain a metabolism that lets you eat a proper diet without gaining weight. According to my friend, Dr. Daniel

Kosich, it is likely that our resting metabolic rate burns at least 20 to 30 more calories (84 to 126 more kilojoules) a day for every 500g (1 lb) of muscle we add through strength training.

Let me say it again, because too many women (in particular) concentrate their exercise time on aerobics and forget about strength training: Muscles are very important for health as well as for aesthetic reasons.

Exercise Aerobically

Aerobic activity requires you to use your larger leg and arm muscles over a sustained period of time, which causes large amounts of oxygen-carrying blood to be pumped to your heart and your cells. Stored body fat can be burned only in the presence of oxygen, so it is this fat that is the source of energy during aerobic activity. To be effective, an aerobics programme should entail a minimum of two 10-minute sessions a day or one 20-minute session a day, at least 4 days a week.

Put It All Together

Recent research suggests that the most effective way to lose body fat is to combine vigorous aerobic exercise with strength training, 2 to 4 days a week, and eat low-fat, moderate-calorie meals. Though you may consume more calories than a person who does not exercise, you will not gain weight and will have less fat and more muscle.

See the Resources Guide on page 240 for some exercise videos that can help motivate you and keep you on track.

One of the complaints about exercise I hear most often from people is that they don't have time. But there are many simple ways you can make exercise part of your daily routine. When shopping or running errands by car, park at the farthest corner of the car park. Don't take the car for nearby errands. Use stairs instead of elevators and escalators. Make dates to walk or bike after work. Most important of all, *write down exercise sessions as appointments.*

Erase Exercise Myths

Put to rest these *misunderstandings* about exercise.

✳ **Myth: You can spot-reduce.** Contrary to popular belief, it is basically impossible to exercise a specific part of your body to lose fat stored there. When you reduce by cutting calories or exercising more, fat is mobilized out of *all* the fat cells *all over the body*.

✳ **Myth: You can sweat off fat.** Sweating is water loss. This will quickly be replaced when you take a drink – which you must do for good health.

✳ **Myth: Muscles lock in fat.** Fat is subcutaneous – between skin and muscle – rather than between muscle and bone. An increase in your muscle mass through strength training will not somehow lock in your fat.

A Note on Eating Disorders

The eating disorders anorexia nervosa and particularly bulimia nervosa are common throughout the world today. I want to say a few words about the subject in the hope that someone for whom this information is relevant will read it and be helped.

Anorexia and bulimia are illnesses. They are not signs of moral weakness or character flaws. They are not who you are, but something that may have happened to you.

The illness may start in the most innocuous of ways — perhaps as a quick means of losing a few pounds. It progresses, however, until it takes on a life of its own, growing out of control and affecting your health, your moods, your perception, your work and your relationships. Left untreated, an eating disorder can shorten or even end your life.

Over the past few decades, science has shown that eating disorders, like heart disease, result from a complex pattern of risk factors. Researchers still don't know exactly which features are the causes of anorexia and bulimia and which are the results.

What is known, however, is that secrecy and anxiety are your worst enemies. Coming out of the closet about your illness is the first step to recovery, making it harder for you to continue facing your problem alone and harder for you to be covert — while, it is hoped, providing you with the support you need.

It isn't always easy for those close to you to be as understanding about eating disorders as you might like and need them to be. But it's important that you help them try. For that reason, I'd like to recommend "The Famine Within," an excellent, award-winning documentary on the subject (see page 240). I think this film could help those round you gain greater understanding and compassion for those who suffer from distorted body images and eating disorders.

More important still, anyone suffering from an eating disorder needs specialized professional help, starting with a complete medical, psychological and nutritional evaluation. A treatment team that includes a therapist, a physician and a dietitian will create a plan suitable for your particular needs and goals. Your therapist can advise you whether a local self-help group might also be worthwhile for you to join.

How recovery is defined, how long it should take and how difficult it will be all vary from person to person — and, to some extent, among treatment programmes. "Bulimic patients treated with cognitive-behavioral therapy or with anti-depressant medication often stop or greatly reduce their binging within four to six months, with a low rate of relapse over time," says Janice M. Cauwels, author of "Bulimia: The Binge-Purge Compulsion". "But bulimia nervosa is a closed circle in which distortions and miseries lead to severe, imbalanced dieting that causes binge-purging that aggravates the distortions and miseries. Short- or long-term individual, group, family or feminist therapy — or even hospitalization — may help some patients break this cycle at a different point."

See the Resources Guide on page 240 for the names of helpful organizations.

With treatment, a bulimic will learn to recognize and change the thoughts and behaviours that trigger a binge, to express feelings and handle stress better, and to develop a stable, reliable eating structure in which no food is necessarily "forbidden". The further away from the binge-purge disorder the bulimic is able to grow, the easier it gets to eat in a healthy, anxiety-free way. In time, she (or he) can assume a more spontaneous relationship with a variety of foods and with normal weight.

I know because I did.

Breakfast

Suggested Breakfast Menus

Just as so many of our mothers told us years ago, breakfast is the most
important meal of the day. A well-balanced, satisfying breakfast featuring complex
carbohydrates and protein – in the form of whole-grain cereals or breads,
fresh fruits and low fat dairy products – gives us the energy we need to begin
our work and to see the morning through without running the hazard of eating
a sugary or fat-laden snack that could derail our healthy eating goals. Use the menus
shown here and the recipes on the following pages as your guide to composing a
breakfast that not only meets your nutritional requirements but also is
easy to make and incomparably delicious.

Poached Fruit with
Cinnamon Yogurt Topping
page 36

Almond Biscotti
page 215

Skinny Café Mocha
page 179

Almond Gelatine Squares in Fruit
page 39

2 slices wholewheat toast
with 1 teaspoon margarine

coffee or tea

Summer Fruit
in Rosemary Syrup
page 40

Pumpkin Spice Bread
page 231

125 ml (4 fl oz) grapefruit juice

Nutritional Analysis per Serving: Calories 363
(Kilojoules 1,540); Total fat 5g; Saturated fat 1g;
Protein 11g; Cholesterol 30mg; Carbohydrates 74g;
Sodium 227mg; Dietary fibre 3g; Calories from fat 12%

Nutritional Analysis per Serving: Calories 510
(Kilojoules 2,167); Total fat 7g; Saturated fat 1g;
Protein 18g; Cholesterol 3mg; Carbohydrates 96g;
Sodium 580mg; Dietary fibre 8g; Calories from fat 12%

Nutritional Analysis per Serving: Calories 558
(Kilojoules 2,364); Total fat 9g; Saturated fat 2g;
Protein 9g; Cholesterol 60mg; Carbohydrates 117g;
Sodium 400mg; Dietary fibre 5g; Calories from fat 14%

Hearty Granola
page 43

125 ml (4 fl oz) skimmed milk

1 peach

Strawberry-Banana Shake
page 176

Nutritional Analysis per Serving: Calories 616 (Kilojoules 2,605); Total fat 14g; Saturated fat 2g; Protein 18g; Cholesterol 3mg; Carbohydrates 110g; Sodium 119mg; Dietary fibre 9g; Calories from fat 20%

Apple-Raisin Oatmeal
page 44

125 ml (4 fl oz) cranberry juice

Nutritional Analysis per Serving: Calories 301 (Kilojoules 1,281); Total fat 3g; Saturated fat 1g; Protein 6g; Cholesterol 1mg; Carbohydrates 65g; Sodium 49mg; Dietary fibre 3g; Calories from fat 9%

Hot Wheat Cereal with Gingered Peaches
page 47

125 ml (4 fl oz) apple juice

Nutritional Analysis per Serving: Calories 324 (Kilojoules 1,385); Total fat 1g; Saturated fat 0g; Protein 6g; Cholesterol 0mg; Carbohydrates 76g; Sodium 13mg; Dietary fibre 3g; Calories from fat 3%

Irish Oatmeal
page 48

*125 g (4 oz)
virtually no fat yogurt with
½ banana*

125 ml (4 fl oz) orange juice

Nutritional Analysis per Serving: Calories 351 (Kilojoules 1,491); Total fat 4g; Saturated fat 0g; Protein 12g; Cholesterol 5mg; Carbohydrates 70g; Sodium 624mg; Dietary fibre 4g; Calories from fat 10%

Blueberry Muffins
page 51

Sunshine Smoothie
page 176

coffee or tea

Nutritional Analysis per Serving: Calories 232 (Kilojoules 986); Total fat 3g; Saturated fat 1g; Protein 8g; Cholesterol 2mg; Carbohydrates 48g; Sodium 344mg; Dietary fibre 3g; Calories from fat 12%

Banana Bread
page 52

½ grapefruit

coffee or tea

Nutritional Analysis per Serving: Calories 314 (Kilojoules 1,335); Total fat 1g; Saturated fat 0g; Protein 6g; Cholesterol 0mg; Carbohydrates 75g; Sodium 380mg; Dietary fibre 3g; Calories from fat 3%

Cranberry Pecan Scones
page 55

1 orange

Hot Cocoa
page 179

Nutritional Analysis per Serving: Calories 560 (Kilojoules 2,376); Total fat 10g; Saturated fat 2g; Protein 17g; Cholesterol 6mg; Carbohydrates 107g; Sodium 659mg; Dietary fibre 6g; Calories from fat 16%

Apple Walnut Bread
page 56

1 banana

coffee or tea

Nutritional Analysis per Serving: Calories 378 (Kilojoules 1,593); Total fat 8g; Saturated fat 1g; Protein 7g; Cholesterol 30mg; Carbohydrates 74g; Sodium 341mg; Dietary fibre 5g; Calories from fat 19%

Cherry Cheese Ring
page 59

1 apple

Hot Fruit Cider
page 180

Nutritional Analysis per Serving: Calories 462 (Kilojoules 1,966); Total fat 5g; Saturated fat 1g; Protein 12g; Cholesterol 2mg; Carbohydrates 96g; Sodium 290mg; Dietary fibre 5g; Calories from fat 10%

Blueberry Coffee Cake
page 60

Cranberry Apple Sauce
page 212

coffee or tea

Nutritional Analysis per Serving: Calories 523 (Kilojoules 2,223); Total fat 6g; Saturated fat 1g; Protein 9g; Cholesterol 2mg; Carbohydrates 116g; Sodium 373mg; Dietary fibre 6g; Calories from fat 10%

*Oat Buttermilk Pancakes
with Honey Fruit Sauce*
page 63

125 ml (4 fl oz) cranberry juice

Nutritional Analysis per Serving: Calories 642 (Kilojoules 2,726); Total fat 6g; Saturated fat 1g; Protein 11g; Cholesterol 2mg; Carbohydrates 146g; Sodium 551mg; Dietary fibre 4g; Calories from fat 8%

*Lemon Poppy Seed Pancakes
with 2 tablespoons maple syrup*
page 64

1 nectarine

coffee or tea

Nutritional Analysis per Serving: Calories 440 (Kilojoules 1,876); Total fat 2g; Saturated fat 0g; Protein 10g; Cholesterol 2mg; Carbohydrates 103g; Sodium 600mg; Dietary fibre 4g; Calories from fat 4%

Very Berry Waffles
with 2 tablespoons maple syrup
page 67

Sunshine Smoothie
page 176

coffee or tea

Nutritional Analysis per Serving: Calories 470 (Kilojoules 1,999); Total fat 6g; Saturated fat 1g; Protein 14g; Cholesterol 3mg; Carbohydrates 99g; Sodium 754mg; Dietary fibre 6g; Calories from fat 11%

Multi-grain Pancakes
page 68

Honey Mint Fruit Compôte
page 231

125 ml (4 fl oz) grapefruit juice

Nutritional Analysis per Serving: Calories 411 (Kilojoules 1,740); Total fat 6g; Saturated fat 1g; Protein 12g; Cholesterol 3mg; Carbohydrates 84g; Sodium 592mg; Dietary fibre 6g; Calories from fat 13%

Santa Fe Eggs
page 71

1 slice multi-grain toast
with 1 teaspoon margarine

125 ml (4 fl oz) orange juice

Nutritional Analysis per Serving: Calories 470 (Kilojoules 1,994); Total fat 14g; Saturated fat 4g; Protein 28g; Cholesterol 241mg; Carbohydrates 58g; Sodium 415mg; Dietary fibre 8g; Calories from fat 27%

Green Pepper Sweetcorn Frittata
page 72

½ toasted English muffin
with 2 teaspoons low fat soft cheese

Strawberry Banana Shake
page 176

Nutritional Analysis per Serving: Calories 424 (Kilojoules 1,789); Total fat 10g; Saturated fat 3g; Protein 19g; Cholesterol 122mg; Carbohydrates 69g; Sodium 801mg; Dietary fibre 4g; Calories from fat 21%

Onion Mushroom Omelet
page 75

1 slice wholewheat toast
with 1 teaspoon margarine

¼ cantaloupe

coffee or tea

Nutritional Analysis per Serving: Calories 315 (Kilojoules 1,329); Total fat 10g; Saturated fat 2g; Protein 16g; Cholesterol 0mg; Carbohydrates 40g; Sodium 999mg; Dietary fibre 6g; Calories from fat 28%

Eggs Benedict
with Low Fat Hollandaise
page 76

Rosemary Roasted Potatoes
page 202

185 g (6 oz) watermelon
chunks

coffee or tea

Nutritional Analysis per Serving: Calories 601 (Kilojoules 2,537); Total fat 18g; Saturated fat 3g; Protein 27g; Cholesterol 291mg; Carbohydrates 88g; Sodium 687mg; Dietary fibre 4g; Calories from fat 27%

Poached Fruit with Cinnamon Yogurt Topping

375 ml (12 fl oz) orange juice

60 ml (2 fl oz) water

1 tablespoon sugar

1 tablespoon raspberry or strawberry
all-fruit preserves

2 teaspoons grated fresh root ginger

4 whole cloves

1 vanilla pod, 4 cm (1½ in) long

2 oranges, peeled and segmented

250 g (8 oz) strawberries,
stemmed and cored

Cinnamon Yogurt Topping

250 g (8 oz) virtually no fat
plain yogurt

1 tablespoon sugar

1 teaspoon vanilla essence

1 teaspoon ground cinnamon

Shopping Tip

* All-fruit preserves are the type sweetened with fruit juice rather than added sugar.

*Preparation: 15 minutes * Cooking: 15 minutes * Serves 4*

Warm fruit with a dollop of spiced yogurt is the ideal comfort food to begin a chilly spring morning. Satisfying the requirement of 2 fruit servings for the entire day, it gets your healthy eating plan off to a good start.

* In a medium saucepan over a high heat, combine the orange juice, water, sugar, preserves, ginger, cloves and vanilla pod. Bring to the boil, then reduce the heat to low and simmer until the liquid thickens, about 10 minutes. Remove the vanilla pod, slice open and scrape out the seeds and return the seeds and split bean to the orange juice mixture.

* Add the orange segments and strawberries. Increase the heat to medium-high and return to the boil. Reduce the heat to medium-low and simmer until fruit is tender, about 2 minutes. Remove from the heat. Remove and discard the cloves and vanilla pod.

* To serve, divide the mixture amongst 4 individual bowls. Top each with an equal amount of the Cinnamon Yogurt Topping.

Cinnamon Yogurt Topping

* In a medium bowl, combine the yogurt, sugar, vanilla and cinnamon, then whisk until blended.

Nutritional Analysis per Serving

Calories 159 (Kilojoules 676); Total fat 1g; Saturated fat 0g; Protein 5g; Cholesterol 3mg; Carbohydrates 35g; Sodium 70mg; Dietary fibre 2g; Calories from fat 4%

Almond Gelatine Squares in Fruit

4 teaspoons unflavoured gelatine

125 ml (4 fl oz) cold water

375 ml (12 fl oz) boiling water

90 g (3 oz) skimmed milk powder

125 g (4 oz) sugar

1 teaspoon almond essence

¼ teaspoon ground cinnamon

1 pear, peeled, cored and cubed

185 g (6 oz) seedless red grapes

2 kiwifruits, peeled and sliced

1 orange, peeled and sectioned

250 g (8 oz) pineapple chunks

60 ml (2 fl oz) orange juice

Nutrition Tip

✳ Kiwifruits, oranges and pineapples are all excellent sources of vitamin C.

Preparation: 15 minutes ✳ *Chilling: 1 hour* ✳ *Serves 4*

If you are short of time in the morning, make the gelatine the night before. The next morning, you'll need only a few minutes to toss the almond-laced gelatine squares with the mixed fruit.

✳ In a small saucepan, combine the gelatine and cold water. Add the boiling water and stir until the gelatine is completely dissolved. Place over a medium heat and bring to the boil, stirring constantly. Gradually whisk in the dry milk and sugar and return to the boil. Stir in the almond essence and cinnamon. When the cinnamon is dissolved, pour the mixture into a 20 cm (8 inch) square pan. Cover and refrigerate until firm, about 1 hour.

✳ In a large bowl, combine the pear, grapes, kiwifruits, orange, pineapple and orange juice. Gently toss to mix well.

✳ To serve, cut the gelatine into 2.5 cm (1 in) squares, add to the fruit and toss gently. Divide amongst 4 individual bowls.

Nutritional Analysis per Serving

Calories 317 (Kilojoules 1,352); Total fat 1g; Saturated fat 0g; Protein 12g; Cholesterol 3mg; Carbohydrates 70g; Sodium 143mg; Dietary fibre 3g; Calories from fat 1.5%

125 g (4 oz) raspberries

125 g (4 oz) blueberries

1 peach, stoned and sliced

1 pear, cored and sliced

250 ml (8 fl oz) water

125 ml (4 fl oz) apple juice

60 ml (2 fl oz) raspberry
vinegar

60 g (2 oz) sugar

5 fresh rosemary sprigs

2 tablespoons finely grated
lemon rind

Storage Tip

* If making the sauce ahead, store in an airtight container in the refrigerator and reheat in a small saucepan over a low heat. The sauce is also delicious chilled.

Summer Fruit in Rosemary Syrup

Preparation: 15 minutes ✳ *Cooking: 15 minutes* ✳ *Serves 4*

Rosemary, the symbolic herb of remembrance, lends its pungent flavour and aroma to this colourful fruit mix. Both the leaves and the pale purple flowers are edible. Be sure to crush the needlelike leaves to release their oils as you add the herb to the saucepan.

✳ Divide the raspberries, blueberries, peach slices and pear slices amongst 4 individual bowls.

✳ To make the rosemary syrup, in a small saucepan over a medium-high heat, combine the water, apple juice, vinegar, sugar, rosemary and lemon rind. Bring to the boil, reduce the heat to low and simmer until the liquid is reduced by half, about 10 minutes. Cool for 5 minutes. Strain the syrup through a fine sieve.

✳ To serve, pour an equal amount of the rosemary syrup over each bowl of fruit.

Nutritional Analysis per Serving

Calories 117 (Kilojoules 497); Total fat 0g; Saturated fat 0g; Protein 1g; Cholesterol 0mg; Carbohydrates 29g; Sodium 5mg; Dietary fibre 3g; Calories from fat 2%

90 g (3 oz) raisins

60 g (2 oz) dried prunes, chopped

60 g (2 oz) dried apples, chopped

60 g (2 oz) dried apricots, chopped

250 ml (8 fl oz) hot water

270 g (9 oz) rolled oats

125 g (4 oz) unsweetened
puffed rice cereal

60 g (2 oz) raw sunflower seeds

60 g (2 oz) flaked almonds

30 g (1 oz) dried skimmed milk
powder

2 tablespoons desiccated coconut

2 tablespoons honey

1 teaspoon ground cinnamon

Hearty Granola

Preparation: 25 minutes ✳ *Cooking: 1 hour* ✳ *Makes 7 cups*

Ted is a big granola fan and really likes this version. It's great with milk as a breakfast cereal, plain as a snack or sprinkled over yogurt as a dessert. Consider making several batches and filling decorative airtight jars to give as gifts. Include a copy of the nutritional analysis and inspire others to take the road to healthy eating.

✳ Preheat the oven to 130°C (250°F/Gas ½).

✳ In a small bowl, soak the raisins and dried fruit in the hot water until softened, 15 minutes. In a large bowl, combine the oats, rice cereal, sunflower seeds, almonds, dry milk, coconut, honey and cinnamon. Add the raisins and fruit with the soaking water. Stir to mix well.

✳ Spread the mixture on a baking sheet and bake for 1 hour, stirring every 15 minutes to prevent sticking and to ensure even baking. Remove from the oven and cool. One serving is 185 g (6 oz).

✳ To store, place in an airtight container for up to one week.

Nutritional Analysis per Serving

Calories 434 (Kilojoules 1,832); Total fat 14g; Saturated fat 2g; Protein 12g; Cholesterol 1mg; Carbohydrates 70g; Sodium 38mg; Dietary fibre 6.5g; Calories from fat 28%

600 ml (1 pint) non–alcoholic apple
  cider or apple juice
45 g (1½ oz) raisins
1 apple, peeled, cored and diced
¾ teaspoon ground cinnamon
135 g (4½ oz) rolled oats
125 g (4 oz) virtually no fat
  plain yogurt
1 teaspoon grated nutmeg

Apple-Raisin Oatmeal

Preparation: 10 minutes ✳ *Cooking: 10 minutes* ✳ *Serves 4*

When I was about 10 years old, I had an exam at school that was very important. That morning I ate a big bowl of hot oatmeal, something I was not accustomed to doing. I did great on the exam and began calling oatmeal "brain food". Now I know that my childhood instincts were remarkably accurate. A hearty breakfast of complex carbohydrates like those found in oatmeal increases your attention span and ability to concentrate. I still eat it whenever I have something important to do.

✳ In a medium saucepan over a medium-high heat, bring the cider or juice to the boil. Stir in the raisins, apple and cinnamon, reduce the heat to low and simmer for 2 minutes. Stir in the oats, increase the heat to medium-high and bring to the boil. Reduce the heat to low and simmer, stirring frequently, until the liquid is absorbed and the oats are creamy, about 6 minutes.

✳ To serve, divide amongst 4 individual bowls. Top each with an equal amount of the yogurt and nutmeg.

Nutritional Analysis per Serving

Calories 243 (Kilojoules 1,036); Total fat 3.5g; Saturated fat 1g; Protein 6g; Cholesterol 1mg; Carbohydrates 50g; Sodium 40mg; Dietary fibre 3g; Calories from fat 13%

Hot Wheat Cereal with Gingered Peaches

*Preparation: 5 minutes * Cooking: 15 minutes * Serves 4*

1 litre (1¾ pints) water

185 g (6 oz) enriched farina
   wheat cereal

375 ml (12 fl oz) apple juice

1 tablespoon grated fresh root ginger

4 peaches, peeled, stoned and sliced

60 ml (2 fl oz) raspberry
   vinegar

3 tablespoons honey

½ teaspoon ground cinnamon

12 blackberries

Notice that this creamy white cereal with warm fruit has no cholesterol and derives just 2 per-cent of its calories from fat. It makes a good alternative to oatmeal for a hot breakfast cereal and provides a grain and a fruit serving, essential components of your daily food needs. If you can't find farina cereal in your supermarket, look in Italian food stores.

* In a medium saucepan over a medium-high heat, bring the water to the boil. Stir in the wheat cereal, reduce the heat to low and simmer, stirring frequently, until thickened, about 10 minutes.

* To make the gingered peaches, in a small saucepan over a high heat, combine the apple juice, ginger and peaches. Bring to the boil, reduce the heat to low and simmer until the liquid is reduced by half, about 10 minutes. Add the vinegar, honey and cinnamon. Increase the heat to medium-high, bring to the boil, reduce the heat to low and simmer until the peaches are tender, about 5 minutes.

* To serve, divide the cereal amongst 4 individual bowls. Top each with an equal amount of the gingered peaches and blackberries.

Nutritional Analysis per Serving

Calories 276 (Kilojoules 1,180); Total fat 1g; Saturated fat 0g; Protein 6g; Cholesterol 0mg; Carbohydrates 64g; Sodium 11mg; Dietary fibre 3g; Calories from fat 3.5%

1 litre (1½ pints) water

1 teaspoon salt

185 g (6 oz) oatmeal

4 teaspoons brown sugar

Nutrition Tip

✳ Try gradually decreasing the amount of salt each time you make oatmeal. The oat flavour is rich and full without a lot of added sodium.

Irish Oatmeal

Preparation: 5 minutes ✳ Cooking: 30 minutes ✳ Serves 4

Karen Averitt serves this nearly every morning at our Montana ranch. It offers a great start to our busy days filled with outdoor activities. It has a wonderfully hearty, chewy texture.

✳ In a medium saucepan over a medium-high heat, combine the water and salt. Bring to the boil. Gradually add the oats, stirring constantly. Reduce the heat to low and simmer, stirring frequently, until the water is absorbed and the oatmeal is creamy, about 30 minutes.

✳ To serve, divide amongst 4 individual bowls. Top each with an equal amount of the brown sugar.

Nutritional Analysis per Serving

Calories 207 (Kilojoules 878); Total fat 4g; Saturated fat 0g; Protein 6g; Cholesterol 0mg; Carbohydrates 40g; Sodium 508mg; Dietary fibre 3g; Calories from fat 17.5%

315 g (10 oz) plus 3 tablespoons
    unbleached plain flour

235 g (7½ oz) wholewheat flour

105 g (3½ oz) plus 3 tablespoons
    brown sugar

1 tablespoon baking powder

1½ teaspoons bicarbonate of soda

½ teaspoon salt

1 teaspoon finely grated lemon rind

580 ml (19 fl oz) buttermilk

1 tablespoon vegetable oil

1½ teaspoons vanilla essence

250 g (8 oz) blueberries

3 tablespoons quick-cooking
    rolled oats

1½ tablespoons margarine

Shopping Tip

✳ Look for fresh blueberries at the height of summer. Chose firm, plump berries and remove any stalks before use. Large berries have more flavour than small ones. If using frozen or canned blueberries, seek brands packed in water rather than a sugary syrup, and drain and blot off all excess liquid.

Blueberry Muffins

Preparation: 25 minutes ✳ *Cooking: 20 minutes* ✳ *Serves 18*

The crunchy topping adds texture – and extra fibre – to these muffins. The recipe makes enough for several breakfasts and healthy midday snacks.

✳ Preheat the oven to 200°C (400°F/Gas 6). Coat tins for 18 muffins with non-stick cooking spray (or line with paper muffin cups).

✳ In a large bowl, combine the 315 g (10 oz) unbleached plain flour, wholewheat flour, 105 g (3½ oz) brown sugar, baking powder, bicarbonate of soda, salt and lemon rind. Make a well in the centre of the dry ingredients. In a medium bowl, whisk together the buttermilk, oil and vanilla. Pour the buttermilk mixture into the well in the dry ingredients and stir until just blended. Fold in the blueberries. Spoon the batter into the prepared muffin tins.

✳ To make the topping, in a small bowl, combine the oats, remaining plain flour, remaining brown sugar and margarine and stir to blend. Sprinkle an equal amount of topping over each muffin.

✳ Bake the muffins until golden brown and a cocktail stick inserted in the centre of a middle muffin comes out clean, about 20 minutes. Cool for 10 minutes.

✳ To serve, arrange on a serving plate. One serving is one muffin. Store wrapped individually in cling film in an airtight container in the freezer for up to 3 months.

Nutritional Analysis per Serving

Calories 172 (Kilojoules 730); Total fat 2g; Saturated fat 0.5g; Protein 5g; Cholesterol 1mg; Carbohydrates 36g; Sodium 295mg; Dietary fibre 2g; Calories from fat 12%

315 g (10 oz) unbleached plain flour

2 teaspoons baking powder

½ teaspoon bicarbonate of soda

½ teaspoon salt

4 large, overripe bananas

2 egg whites

185 g (6 oz) sugar

60 ml (2 fl oz) buttermilk

1 teaspoon vanilla essence

Shopping Tip

✳ Bananas are grown in South and Central America and are shipped throughout the world. Often picked while still green, they continue to ripen after harvesting. Purchase plump specimens with unblemished skins. Stored at room temperature, the fruit will ripen in 2 to 3 days. Ripe bananas are uniformly yellow, speckled with brown spots. They need to be very ripe for use in bread.

Banana Bread

Preparation: 20 minutes ✳ *Cooking: 1 hour* ✳ *Serves 8*

The perfect solution for using bananas that are too ripe to eat out of hand is to make banana bread. Bananas are high in potassium, niacin and vitamins A and C.

✳ Preheat the oven to 180°C (350°F/Gas 4). Coat a 23 x 13 cm (9 x 5 in) loaf tin with non-stick cooking spray.

✳ In a large bowl, combine the flour, baking powder, bicarbonate of soda and salt. Make a well in the centre of the dry ingredients. In a medium bowl, mash the bananas until smooth. Add the egg whites, sugar, buttermilk and vanilla and stir to mix well. Pour the banana mixture into the well in the dry ingredients and fold together until blended.

✳ Pour the batter into the prepared loaf tin and bake until a cocktail stick inserted in the centre comes out clean, 55–60 minutes. Cool for 10 minutes.

✳ To serve, cut into 8 slices. One serving is one slice. Store wrapped in cling film in an airtight container in the freezer for up to 1 month.

Nutritional Analysis per Serving

Calories 290 (Kilojoules 1,234); Total fat 1g; Saturated fat 0g; Protein 5g; Cholesterol 0mg; Carbohydrates 70g; Sodium 378mg; Dietary fibre 2g; Calories from fat 2%

Cranberry Pecan Scones

185 g (6 oz) fresh cranberries

2 tablespoons water

120 g (4 oz) sugar

1 tablespoon brown sugar

315 g (10 oz) unbleached plain flour

2 teaspoons baking powder

½ teaspoon bicarbonate of soda

¼ teaspoon salt

30g (1oz) margarine, cut into
    small pieces

185 ml (6 fl oz) buttermilk

1 egg white

30 g (1 oz) pecans, chopped

Shopping Tip

* Fresh cranberries are available in the
autumn. During other times of the year,
substitute frozen, whole, unsweetened
cranberries or dried cranberries.

Preparation: 20 minutes ✳ *Cooking: 25 minutes* ✳ *Serves 6*

*Cranberries, the fruit of a low-lying vine native to North America, are
a good source of vitamin C and high in fibre.*

✳ Preheat the oven to 200°C (400°F/Gas 6). Coat a baking sheet
with non-stick cooking spray.

✳ In a small saucepan over a medium heat, combine the
cranberries, water and half the sugar. Simmer until the
cranberries are tender and the mixture thickens, about 10 minutes.

✳ In a food processor with the metal blade or by hand in a large
bowl, combine the remaining sugar, brown sugar, flour, baking
powder, bicarbonate of soda and salt. Process or stir to mix well.
Add the margarine and process or use a fork to blend until the
mixture resembles coarse crumbs.

✳ In a small bowl, combine the buttermilk and egg white. Stir
into the flour mixture.

✳ Turn the dough on to a lightly floured work surface and knead
gently for about 5 times. Form into a ball, place on the prepared
baking sheet and press into a 20 cm (8 in) round. Using a lightly
floured knife, cut the round into 12 wedges without cutting
completely through to the baking sheet. Spoon an equal amount
of the cranberry mixture on to the centre of each wedge and
press down gently with the back of the spoon. Top with an equal
amount of the pecans. Bake until golden brown and a cocktail
stick inserted in the centre comes out clean, 13–15 minutes.
Cool for 10 minutes.

✳ To serve, cut into 12 pieces. One serving is 2 scones. Store
wrapped in cling film in the refrigerator for up to 3 days.

Nutritional Analysis per Serving

Calories 359 (Kilojoules 1,520); Total fat 8.5g; Saturated fat 1g; Protein 7g;
Cholesterol 1mg; Carbohydrates 68g; Sodium 461mg; Dietary fibre 3g;
Calories from fat 21%

250 g (8 oz) tart apples, grated

2 tablespoons lemon juice

½ teaspoon finely grated lemon rind

60 g (2 oz) light brown sugar

90 g (3 oz) honey

30 g (1 oz) margarine, melted

2 tablespoons skimmed milk

1 egg

315 g (10 oz) unbleached plain flour

2 teaspoons baking powder

½ teaspoon bicarbonate of soda

1¼ teaspoons ground cinnamon

¼ teaspoon salt

40 g (1⅓ oz) walnuts, chopped

Cooking Tip

✳ For a heartier texture, dice the apples instead of grating them. For an aromatic change of pace, add ¼ teaspoon of ground allspice, nutmeg or ginger along with the cinnamon.

Apple Walnut Bread

Preparation: 20 minutes ✳ *Cooking: 1 hour* ✳ *Serves 8*

Tart apples, including Granny Smiths and pippins, work best for baking. Save sweeter apples, such as Red and Golden Delicious, for eating out of hand. All apples are high in fibre, water and pectin, which helps lower cholesterol levels, and are a good source of vitamin C.

✳ Preheat the oven to 180°C (350°F/Gas 4). Coat a 23 x 13 cm (9 x 5 in) loaf tin with non-stick cooking spray.

✳ In a medium bowl, combine the apples, lemon juice and lemon rind. Stir to mix well. In a large bowl, whisk together the brown sugar, honey, margarine, milk and egg. Stir in the apple mixture. In another large bowl, sift together the flour, baking powder, bicarbonate of soda, cinnamon and salt. Make a well in the centre of the dry ingredients. Pour the apple mixture into the well and fold together until blended. Fold in the walnuts.

✳ Pour the batter into the prepared loaf tin and bake until a cocktail stick inserted in the centre comes out clean, about 1 hour. If it begins to over-brown during cooking, cover the top of the bread with foil. Cool for 10 minutes.

✳ To serve, cut into 8 slices. One serving is one slice. Store in an airtight container in the freezer for up to 3 months.

Nutritional Analysis per Serving

Calories 282 (Kilojoules 1,190); Total fat 8g; Saturated fat 1g; Protein 6g; Cholesterol 30mg; Carbohydrates 50g; Sodium 341mg; Dietary fibre 2g; Calories from fat 25%

Cherry Cheese Ring

2 teaspoons dried yeast

310 ml (10 fl oz) warm water

15g (½ oz) margarine, melted

5 tablespoons sugar

½ teaspoon salt

545 g (17½ oz) unbleached plain
    flour

750 g (1½ lb) cherries, stoned

250 g (8 oz) low fat soft cheese

60 g (2 oz) virtually no fat
    plain yogurt

½ teaspoon vanilla essence

1 tablespoon skimmed milk

Shopping Tip

✳ In winter, substitute 1 kg (2¼ lb)
canned stoned sour cherries in water for
the fresh cherries.

Preparation: 20 minutes ✳ *Cooking: 45 minutes* ✳ *Serves 8*

*In addition to the preparation and cooking times noted above, this dough
needs to rise for 1¾ hours before baking.*

✳ In a large bowl, dissolve the yeast in the water and let stand for 5
minutes. Add the margarine, 3 tablespoons of the sugar, the salt and
flour and work into a dough. Using a mixer with a dough hook or
by hand on a lightly floured work surface, knead the dough until
smooth and elastic, about 4 minutes. Form into a ball. Coat a large
bowl with non-stick cooking spray, add the dough and turn to coat
all sides. Cover with a tea towel and let rise in a warm place, free
from draught, until doubled, about 1 hour.

✳ In a medium saucepan over a medium heat, place the cherries
in water to cover and bring to the boil. Reduce the heat to low
and simmer for 10 minutes. Drain well, blot to remove all excess
liquid and cool.

✳ In a food processor with the metal blade or in a blender,
combine the cheese, yogurt and vanilla and process until smooth.

✳ Punch down the dough and roll out to a 20 x 35 cm (8 x 14
in) rectangle. Spread the cheese mixture over the dough to within
2.5 cm (1 in) of the edges. Top with the cherries. Fold the
dough over lengthways and pinch the edges to seal. Coat a
baking sheet with non-stick cooking spray. On the baking sheet,
form the dough into a ring. Using kitchen scissors, make deep
cuts all round the top of the ring. Cover with a tea towel and let
rise until doubled in bulk, about 45 minutes.

✳ Preheat an oven to 190°C (375°F/Gas 5). Brush the top of the
ring with the milk and sprinkle with the remaining sugar. Bake
until golden brown, about 30 minutes. Cool for 10 minutes.

✳ To serve, cut into 8 pieces. One serving is one piece.

Nutritional Analysis per Serving

Calories 373 (Kilojoules 1,582); Total fat 4.5g; Saturated fat 0.5g;
Protein 12g; Cholesterol 2mg; Carbohydrates 75g; Sodium 280mg;
Dietary fibre 3g; Calories from fat 11%

250 g (8 oz) plus 30g (1 oz) sugar

105 g (3½ oz) brown sugar

250 g (8 oz) low fat soft cream cheese

30g (1 oz) margarine

3 egg whites

1 teaspoon vanilla essence

315 g (10 oz) unbleached plain flour

2 teaspoons baking powder

¼ teaspoon grated nutmeg

¼ teaspoon salt

250 g (8 oz) blueberries

1 teaspoon ground cinnamon

Cooking Tip

✱ Folding is a slightly different technique than simply stirring ingredients to combine them. The purpose of folding a mixture is to add air while incorporating a heavier ingredient into a lighter one. When folding the blueberries into this mixture, for example, use a rubber spatula to cut repeatedly through the batter in a down, across and upwards motion.

Blueberry Coffee Cake

Preparation: 20 minutes ✱ Cooking: 35 minutes ✱ Serves 8

Using egg whites only, rather than the whole eggs, lowers the fat and cholesterol in this coffee cake without sacrificing any of the flavour.

✱ Preheat the oven to 180°C (350°F/Gas 4). Coat a Bundt pan or 23 x 33 cm (9 x 13 in) baking tin with non-stick cooking spray.

✱ To make the cake, in a large bowl using an electric mixer or by hand, beat the 250g (8oz) sugar, brown sugar, cheese and margarine until creamy. Add the egg whites and vanilla and beat until smooth. In a small bowl, combine the flour, baking powder, nutmeg and salt. Stir the flour mixture into the cheese mixture. Fold in the blueberries. Pour the mixture into the prepared tin.

✱ To make the topping, in a small bowl, combine the 2 tablespoons sugar and cinnamon and sprinkle over the mixture.

✱ Bake until a cocktail stick inserted in the centre comes out clean, about 1 hour in a Bundt pan and about 35 minutes in a baking tin. Cool for 10 minutes.

✱ To serve, cut into 8 pieces. One serving is one piece. Store wrapped in cling film in the refrigerator for up to 3 days.

Nutritional Analysis per Serving

Calories 402 (Kilojoules 1,703); Total fat 5.5g; Saturated fat 1g; Protein 9g; Cholesterol 2mg; Carbohydrates 84g; Sodium 368mg; Dietary fibre 2g; Calories from fat 12.5%

375 ml (12 fl oz) buttermilk

65 g (2¼ oz) rolled oats

15g (½ oz) margarine, melted

2 egg whites

½ teaspoon vanilla essence

155 g (5 oz) unbleached plain flour

30g (1 oz) brown sugar

½ teaspoon bicarbonate of soda

½ teaspoon salt

¼ teaspoon grated nutmeg

Honey Fruit Sauce

1 pear, peeled, cored and diced

1 tart apple, peeled, cored and diced

375 g (12 oz) honey

1 tablespoon lemon juice

1 teaspoon finely grated lemon rind

¼ teaspoon ground cinnamon

4 whole cloves

Cooking Tip

✳ Pancakes have the best texture when the mixture is made just before cooking because any storage time causes the bicarbonate of soda to lose its punch.

Oat Buttermilk Pancakes with Honey Fruit Sauce

Preparation: 15 minutes ✳ Cooking: 10 minutes ✳ Serves 4

Rolled oats add texture and fibre to old-fashioned American-style buttermilk pancakes. Prepare the sauce before the pancakes.

✳ In a large bowl, combine the buttermilk, oats, margarine, egg whites and vanilla. Let stand for 10 minutes. In a large bowl, combine the flour, brown sugar, bicarbonate of soda, salt and nutmeg. Add the flour mixture to the buttermilk mixture and stir to mix well.

✳ Coat a griddle or large non-stick frying pan with non-stick cooking spray. Place over a medium-high heat until hot. The griddle is the right temperature when water dropped on the surface bounces and dances. If the water evaporates immediately, the griddle is too hot; if the water sits still, the griddle is not hot enough. Spoon the mixture in scant 75 g (2½ oz) portions on to the hot griddle to make 12 pancakes. Flip each pancake when the surface is covered with tiny bubbles, about 3 minutes. Cook until the bottom is golden brown, about 2 minutes more.

✳ To serve, divide amongst 4 individual plates. One serving is 3 pancakes.

Honey Fruit Sauce

✳ In a small saucepan over a medium heat, combine the pear, apple, honey, lemon juice, lemon rind, cinnamon and cloves. Bring to the boil, then reduce the heat to low and simmer until the fruit is tender, about 5 minutes. Remove and discard the cloves.

✳ To serve, spoon the hot sauce over the pancakes. One serving is 2 tablespoons. Store in an airtight container in the refrigerator for up to 1 week. Reheat before serving

Nutritional Analysis per Serving

Calories 584 (Kilojoules 2,481); Total fat 5.5g; Saturated fat 1g; Protein 11g; Cholesterol 2mg; Carbohydrates 131g; Sodium 542mg; Dietary fibre 3.5g; Calories from fat 9%

235 g (7½ oz) unbleached plain flour

60 g (2 oz) sugar

1 tablespoon poppy seeds

1 teaspoon baking powder

½ teaspoon bicarbonate of soda

¼ teaspoon salt

185 ml (6 fl oz) skimmed milk

60 g (2 oz) virtually no fat plain
   yogurt

2 egg whites

1 tablespoon lemon juice

2 teaspoons finely grated lemon rind

Storage Tip

✳ Poppy seeds contain a lot of oil and go rancid quickly. Store in an airtight container in a cool, dark place for up to 6 months.

Lemon Poppy Seed Pancakes

Preparation: 15 minutes ✳ *Cooking: 10 minutes* ✳ *Serves 4*

Several types of poppy plants provide edible seeds. Some seeds are white; most are black. Both have a slightly sweet, nutty flavour. If desired, lightly toast the seeds before using to bring out more of their distinctive flavour.

✳ In a large bowl, combine the flour, sugar, poppy seeds, baking powder, bicarbonate of soda and salt. Make a well in the centre. In another large bowl, whisk together the milk, yogurt, egg whites, lemon juice and lemon rind. Pour the milk mixture into the well in the flour mixture and stir to mix well.

✳ Coat a griddle or large non-stick frying pan with non-stick cooking spray. Place over a medium-high heat until hot. The griddle is the right temperature when water dropped on the surface bounces and dances. If the water evaporates immediately, the griddle is too hot; if the water sits still, the griddle is not hot enough. Spoon the mixture in scant 75 g (2½ oz) portions on to the hot griddle to make 12 pancakes. Flip each pancake when the surface is covered with tiny bubbles, about 3 minutes. Cook until the bottom is golden brown, about 2 minutes more.

✳ To serve, divide amongst 4 individual plates. One serving is 3 pancakes.

Nutritional Analysis per Serving

Calories 291 (Kilojoules 1,238); Total fat 2g; Saturated fat 0g; Protein 10g; Cholesterol 2mg; Carbohydrates 65g; Sodium 517mg; Dietary fibre 2g; Calories from fat 7%

220 g (7 oz) dried black beans

900 ml (32 fl oz) water

500 g (1 lb) whole plum tomatoes, chopped

140 g (4½ oz) green chillies, chopped

3 teaspoons chilli powder

¾ teaspoon ground cumin

½ teaspoon cocoa

3 tablespoons chopped fresh coriander

¼ teaspoon ground cayenne pepper

4 eggs

30 g (1 oz) reduced-fat Cheddar cheese, grated

2 tablespoons chopped spring onions, green and white parts

Cooking Tip

✳ If purchasing cooked beans for this recipe, you'll need 440 g (14 oz). Be sure to drain and rinse before using. If cooking the beans ahead, cool completely and store in the refrigerator for up to 1 week.

Santa Fe Eggs

Preparation: 10 minutes ✳ *Cooking: 1 hour 25 minutes* ✳ *Serves 4*

Inspired by huevos rancheros, *this dish is reminiscent of the foods I eat when visiting New Mexico. While beans may seem an unlikely breakfast choice, they are a wonderful source of protein and fibre.*

✳ In a large pot over a high heat, combine the beans and water and bring to the boil. Reduce the heat to medium and cook for 1 hour, skimming away the grey foam that appears. Drain well.

✳ In a large non-stick frying pan over a medium heat, combine the beans, tomatoes, chillies, chilli powder, cumin and cocoa. Bring to the boil, reduce the heat to medium-low and simmer until the mixture thickens, about 15 minutes. Stir in the coriander and cayenne. One at a time, break the eggs into a small bowl and carefully slip on top of the simmering liquid. Cover and poach the eggs until they are just cooked, about 7 minutes. Remove from the heat, sprinkle with the cheese, cover and let stand for 1 minute.

✳ To serve, divide amongst 4 individual bowls. Top each with an equal amount of the onions.

Nutritional Analysis per Serving

Calories 310 (Kilojoules 1,309); Total fat 9g; Saturated fat 3g; Protein 25g; Cholesterol 241mg; Carbohydrates 34g; Sodium 165mg; Dietary fibre 6g; Calories from fat 27%

1 teaspoon olive oil

1 onion, sliced

1 large green pepper seeded, cored
    and sliced into thin strips

125 g (4 oz) pimientos
    (sweet peppers), chopped

280 g (9 oz) sweetcorn kernels, well
    drained if canned

½ teaspoon dried oregano

2 eggs

4 egg whites

60 ml (2 fl oz) skimmed milk

¾ teaspoon salt

¼ teaspoon ground black pepper

⅛ teaspoon ground mustard

1 tablespoon grated pecorino cheese

Green Pepper Sweetcorn Frittata

Preparation: 20 minutes ✳ Cooking: 30 minutes ✳ Serves 4

Peppers and sweetcorn are excellent sources of vitamin A, and peppers are rich in the antioxidant vitamin C as well. Both vegetables are in season from late spring through early autumn, giving you plenty of opportunity to make this quick meal over and over again.

✳ Preheat the oven to 180°C (350°F/Gas 4). In a large ovenproof frying pan over medium heat, heat the olive oil. Add the onion and green pepper and cook until tender, about 5 minutes. Add the pimientos, sweetcorn and oregano and cook for 5 minutes. Transfer the vegetables into a medium bowl.

✳ In a large bowl, combine the eggs, egg whites, milk, salt, pepper and mustard and whisk until blended. Add the egg mixture to the vegetable mixture.

✳ In the same frying pan over a low heat, pour in the egg-vegetable mixture. Cook, stirring frequently, until the eggs are firm on the bottom and almost set on the top, 8–10 minutes. Sprinkle the cheese on top and bake in the oven until the eggs are set, 5–8 minutes.

✳ To serve, cut into 4 wedges and divide amongst individual plates.

Nutritional Analysis per Serving

Calories 188 (Kilojoules 793); Total fat 6g; Saturated fat 2g; Protein 11g; Cholesterol 122mg; Carbohydrates 24g; Sodium 705mg; Dietary fibre 2g; Calories from fat 30%

Onion Mushroom Omelet

Preparation: 15 minutes ✳ *Cooking: 15 minutes* ✳ *Serves 1*

Healthy diets don't have to be skimpy, as this hearty omelet shows. Designed as a breakfast dish, this works equally well as a light dinner. Containing just 197 calories per serving and requiring only 15 minutes' preparation time, it's a better choice than most "fast food" options.

1 teaspoon margarine

1 small onion, thinly sliced

2 teaspoons sugar

90 g (3 oz) mushrooms, sliced

1 tablespoon balsamic vinegar

3 egg whites

1 tablespoon skimmed milk

¼ teaspoon salt

⅛ teaspoon ground black pepper

1 tablespoon chopped fresh parsley

Nutrition Tip

✳ All the fat and cholesterol in eggs reside in their yolks, while the egg whites are rich in protein and albumin. For healthier cooking of any recipe with eggs, substitute 2 egg whites for each whole egg.

✳ In a large non-stick frying pan over a medium heat, heat the margarine. Add the onion and sugar and cook until the onion is tender and golden brown, about 4 minutes. Add the mushrooms and vinegar and cook until the mushrooms are tender, about 3 minutes. Transfer the onion mixture to a small bowl.

✳ In a large bowl, combine the egg whites, milk, salt and pepper. Using an electric mixer or by hand, beat until stiff peaks form.

✳ Wipe out the frying pan and coat with non-stick cooking spray. Place over a medium heat; add the egg-white mixture and gently flatten it using the back of a spoon. Spread the onion mixture over half of the eggs. Cover, reduce the heat to medium-low and cook until the eggs are cooked through and the centre of the omelet is set, 4–5 minutes. Using a metal spatula, carefully loosen the underside of the omelet, fold in half, cover and cook for 1 minute more.

✳ To serve, slide the omelet on to a plate and garnish with the parsley. If preparing several omelets, keep the first ones warm, covered with foil, in a 130°C (250°F/Gas ½) oven until all are cooked.

Nutritional Analysis per Serving

Calories 162 (Kilojoules 683); Total fat 5g; Saturated fat 1g; Protein 12g; Cholesterol 0mg; Carbohydrates 19g; Sodium 745mg; Dietary fibre 2g; Calories from fat 27%

60g (2 oz) back bacon, rinded and
    cut into 4 slices

4 eggs

4 English muffins, halved and toasted

½ teaspoon ground paprika

Low Fat Hollandaise

155ml (5 fl oz) evaporated milk

1 egg yolk

¼ teaspoon salt

10g (⅓ oz) margarine

1 tablespoon unbleached plain flour

1 tablespoon lemon juice

Nutrition Tip

✳ To lower the percentage of calories from
fat for your meal as a whole, pair Eggs
Benedict with Rosemary Roasted Potatoes
(recipe on page 202) as outlined in the
Suggested Menu on page 35.

Eggs Benedict with Low Fat Hollandaise

Preparation: 25 minutes ✳ Cooking: 15 minutes ✳ Serves 4

*I'm very fond of eggs Benedict and asked Robin Vitetta to develop a
healthy version. This is the most nutritious recipe we could come up with
that still tastes the way the dish ought to taste. It is still higher in fat than
our healthy goals and for that reason should be eaten as a special-occasion
treat. Consider it for brunch, after an all-fruit breakfast, and plan an
especially low fat dinner that evening.*

✳ Coat a large non-stick frying pan with non-stick cooking spray
and place over a medium heat. Add the bacon and cook until
brown on both sides, 3 minutes. Drain on kitchen paper.

✳ In a medium saucepan over a high heat, bring 10 cm (4 in)
of water to the boil. Reduce the heat to medium-low. One at
a time, break the eggs into a small bowl and carefully slip into
the simmering water. Poach until the whites are cooked
through, 3–5 minutes.

✳ To serve, stack 2 English muffin halves on 4 individual plates.
Top each stack with 1 slice of bacon. Using a slotted spoon, place
an egg on top of the bacon. Top each with an equal amount of the
Low Fat Hollandaise and paprika.

Low Fat Hollandaise

✳ In a small bowl, whisk together the milk, egg yolk and salt.
In a non-stick frying pan over a medium heat, heat the margarine.
Gradually whisk in the flour, reduce the heat to low and cook,
stirring constantly, until smooth and bubbly, about 3 minutes.

✳ Increase the heat to medium. Gradually add the milk mixture,
stirring constantly, and bring to the boil. Reduce the heat to low
and simmer, stirring constantly, until thick and bubbly, about 1
minute. Remove from the heat and stir in the lemon juice.

Nutritional Analysis per Serving

Calories 402 (Kilojoules 1,691); Total fat 17g; Saturated fat 3g; Protein 22g;
Cholesterol 291mg; Carbohydrates 43g; Sodium 671mg; Dietary fibre 1.5g;
Calories from fat 38%

Lunch

Suggested Lunch Menus

With the busy lives so many of us lead today, lunch all too often gets short shrift as
a quickly eaten fast-food meal. That's a shame, because mid-day is the time for
most efficiently supplying our bodies with the proteins we need, accompanied by complex
carbohydrates for sustained energy. The menus shown here and the recipes on the pages
that follow, however, demonstrate how simple it can be to prepare your own healthy lunch
that is easy to eat, completely satisfying and full of foods that are high in flavour
and low in fat. Many of them also pack easily, allowing you to enjoy a healthy
meal even in the midst of the most hectic day.

Louisiana Crab Gumbo
page 84

Caponata
page 189

1 apple

250 ml (8 fl oz) fresh lemonade

Nutritional Analysis per Serving: Calories 539
(Kilojoules 2,281); Total fat 13g; Saturated fat 2g;
Protein 33g; Cholesterol 68mg; Carbohydrates 77g;
Sodium 1115mg; Dietary fibre 13g; Calories from fat 22%

Turkey Vegetable Gumbo
page 87

1 wholewheat roll

1 pear

herbal iced tea

Nutritional Analysis per Serving: Calories 377
(Kilojoules 1,592); Total fat 5g; Saturated fat 1g;
Protein 19g; Cholesterol 22mg; Carbohydrates 67g;
Sodium 774mg; Dietary fibre 12g; Calories from fat 12%

Hearty Vegetable Stew
page 88

Mushroom-Topped Crostini
page 190

*30 g (1 oz) blackberries
and ¼ cantaloupe melon*

mineral water

Nutritional Analysis per Serving: Calories 397
(Kilojoules 1,676); Total fat 8g; Saturated fat 1g;
Protein 14g; Cholesterol 0mg; Carbohydrates 70g;
Sodium 885mg; Dietary fibre 11g; Calories from fat 18%

*Chicken Soup
with Parsley Dumplings*
page 91

*1 carrot and 1 celery stalk
with Chive Chutney Dip*
page 186

*185 ml (6 fl oz) cranberry juice
with 60 ml (2 fl oz) seltzer water*

Nutritional Analysis per Serving: Calories 570
(Kilojoules 2,401); Total fat 10g; Saturated fat 1g;
Protein 42g; Cholesterol 77mg; Carbohydrates 82g;
Sodium 1,080mg; Dietary fibre 6g; Calories from fat 16%

Black Bean Soup
page 92

Chilli-Cheese Corn Bread
page 193

Iced Fruit Cider
page 180

Nutritional Analysis per Serving: Calories 696
(Kilojoules 2,929); Total fat 10g; Saturated fat 3g;
Protein 35g; Cholesterol 12mg; Carbohydrates 118g;
Sodium 557mg; Dietary fibre 11g; Calories from fat 13%

Pasta and Watercress Soup
page 95

*2 slices wholewheat bread
with 2 teaspoons low fat soft cheese*

1 peach

250 ml (8 fl oz) grape juice

Nutritional Analysis per Serving: Calories 683
(Kilojoules 2,742); Total fat 8g; Saturated fat 2g;
Protein 22g; Cholesterol 0mg; Carbohydrates 120g;
Sodium 550mg; Dietary fibre 12g; Calories from fat 10%

Potato Soup
page 96

2 slices dark rye bread

1 orange

mineral water

Nutritional Analysis per Serving: Calories 373
(Kilojoules 1,580); Total fat 5g; Saturated fat 1g;
Protein 15mg; Cholesterol 3mg; Carbohydrates 71g;
Sodium 657g; Dietary fibre 9g; Calories from fat 12%

Shredded Chicken Sandwich
page 99

*40 g (2 oz) mixed greens
with Mustard Vinaigrette*
page 184

1 nectarine

250 ml (8 fl oz) lemonade

Nutritional Analysis per Serving: Calories 468
(Kilojoules 1,986); Total fat 4g; Saturated fat 1g;
Protein 40mg; Cholesterol 88mg; Carbohydrates 72g;
Sodium 979g; Dietary fibre 7g; Calories from fat 8%

*Spicy Chicken Burgers
with Creamy Horseradish*
page 100

*1 tomato and ½ cucumber sliced
with Dill Dressing*
page 183

¼ honeydew melon

*185 ml (6 fl oz) orange juice
with 60 ml (2 fl oz) seltzer water*

Nutritional Analysis per Serving: Calories 534
(Kilojoules 2,253); Total fat 10g; Saturated fat 6g;
Protein 42g; Cholesterol 111mg; Carbohydrates 68g;
Sodium 605mg; Dietary fibre 7g; Calories from fat 17%

*Turkey Burgers
with Mushroom Sauce*
page 103

*60 g (2 oz) mixed greens
with Basil Dressing*
page 183

*185 g (6 oz)
watermelon chunks*

Tangy Tomato Drink
page 180

Nutritional Analysis per Serving: Calories 492
(Kilojoules 2,082); Total fat 12g; Saturated fat 7g;
Protein 42g; Cholesterol 100mg; Carbohydrates 55g;
Sodium 1115mg; Dietary fibre 3g; Calories from fat 22%

Tuna Salad Sandwich
page 104

*125 g (4 oz) virtually no fat
plain yogurt*

60 g (2 oz) strawberries

Iced Skinny Café Mocha
page 179

Nutritional Analysis per Serving: Calories 377
(Kilojoules 1,601); Total fat 4g; Saturated fat 2g;
Protein 38g; Cholesterol 55mg; Carbohydrates 52g;
Sodium 786mg; Dietary fibre 4g; Calories from fat 10%

Tomato-Basil Pizza
page 107

185 g (6 oz) green grapes

8 fl oz (250 ml) grapefruit juice

Nutritional Analysis per Serving: Calories 757
(Kilojoules 3,202); Total fat 17g; Saturated fat 3g;
Protein 22g; Cholesterol 8mg; Carbohydrates 138g;
Sodium 745mg; Dietary fibre 9g; Calories from fat 20%

Mushroom Cheese Pizza
page 108

¼ cantaloupe

250 ml (8 fl oz) apple juice

Nutritional Analysis per Serving: Calories 624
(Kilojoules 2,646); Total fat 13g; Saturated fat 3g;
Protein 19g; Cholesterol 8mg; Carbohydrates 114g;
Sodium 602mg; Dietary fibre 9g; Calories from fat 19%

Ted's Favourite Pizza
page 111

Tangy Tomato Drink
page 180

Nutritional Analysis per Serving: Calories 864
(Kilojoules 3,648); Total fat 31g; Saturated fat 14g;
Protein 52g; Cholesterol 83mg; Carbohydrates 101g;
Sodium 2,132mg; Dietary fibre 12g; Calories from fat 32%

Greek Salad
page 112

Oven-baked French Fries
page 202

1 apple

mineral water

Nutritional Analysis per Serving: Calories 433
(Kilojoules 1,822); Total fat 16g; Saturated fat 6g;
Protein 28g; Cholesterol 58mg; Carbohydrates 47g;
Sodium 811mg; Dietary fibre 6g; Calories from fat 33%

Taco Salad
with Avocado Dressing
page 115

1 carrot

4 Kalamata olives

*125 ml (4 fl oz) orange juice
with 125 ml (4 fl oz) seltzer water*

Nutritional Analysis per Serving: Calories 415
(Kilojoules 1,744); Total fat 17g; Saturated fat 6g;
Protein 9g; Cholesterol 22mg; Carbohydrates 58g;
Sodium 542mg; Dietary fibre 6g; Calories from fat 36%

Lentil and Smoked Turkey Salad
page 116

2 flatbread biscuits

1 orange

250 ml (8 fl oz) grapefruit juice

Nutritional Analysis per Serving: Calories 603
(Kilojoules 2,553); Total fat 7g; Saturated fat 1g;
Protein 40g; Cholesterol 38mg; Carbohydrates 100g;
Sodium 742mg; Dietary fibre 10g; Calories from fat 10%

Curried Chicken, Rice
and Spinach Salad
page 119

2 sesame breadsticks

90 g (3 oz) green grapes

Tangy Tomato Drink
page 180

Nutritional Analysis per Serving: Calories 547
(Kilojoules 2,311); Total fat 6g; Saturated fat 1g;
Protein 46g; Cholesterol 88mg; Carbohydrates 79g;
Sodium 1,340mg; Dietary fibre 11g; Calories from fat 10%

Orzo, Sun-Dried Tomato
and Pea Salad
page 120

5 melba toast crackers
with Creamy Spinach Spread
page 186

*185 g (6 oz)
pineapple chunks*

250 ml (8 fl oz) lemonade

Nutritional Analysis per Serving: Calories 600
(Kilojoules 2,533); Total fat 10g; Saturated fat 3g;
Protein 23g; Cholesterol 15mg; Carbohydrates 108g;
Sodium 445mg; Dietary fibre 11g; Calories from fat 15%

Tabbouleh
page 123

Chilli-Cheese Corn Bread
page 193

1 apple

Iced Fruit Cider
page 180

Nutritional Analysis per Serving: Calories 602
(Kilojoules 2,529); Total fat 15g; Saturated fat 2g;
Protein 15g; Cholesterol 3mg; Carbohydrates 103g;
Sodium 678mg; Dietary fibre 13g; Calories from fat 22%

Greens and Peppers Salad
page 124

Hummus with Pitta Bread
page 190

mineral water

Nutritional Analysis per Serving: Calories 591
(Kilojoules 2,499); Total fat 12g; Saturated fat 4g;
Protein 32g; Cholesterol 14mg; Carbohydrates 94g;
Sodium 825g; Dietary fibre 16g; Calories from fat 18%

Louisiana Crab Gumbo

2 teaspoons vegetable oil

1 large onion, chopped

3 garlic cloves, very finely chopped

2 celery stalks, sliced

1 green pepper, seeded, cored and chopped

375 ml (12 fl oz) Chicken Stock (recipe on page 206) or canned reduced sodium chicken broth

3 large tomatoes, peeled, seeded and diced

250 ml (8 fl oz) bottled clam juice

1 tablespoon chopped fresh oregano

1 bay leaf

¼ teaspoon hot pepper sauce

¼ teaspoon ground black pepper

375 g (12 oz) okra, sliced

375 g (12 oz) cooked, shredded crabmeat, picked over to remove shells

185 g (6 oz) sweetcorn kernels

Preparation: 20 minutes ✳ *Cooking: 25 minutes* ✳ *Serves 4*

Okra, native to Africa, is used extensively in Creole cooking. In fact, the term gumbo is derived from an African word for the plant. The slender, ribbed or smooth, fuzzy, green pods are 2.5–7.5 cm (2–3 in) long and have a mild flavour resembling that of green beans. Okra can be blanched and served cold in salads, sautéed and served as a side dish or used as a thickener in soups and stews.

✳ In a large saucepan over a medium heat, heat the oil. Add the onion, garlic, celery and green pepper and sauté until tender, about 5 minutes.

✳ Add the stock or broth, tomatoes, clam juice, oregano, bay leaf, hot sauce and pepper and bring to the boil. Add the okra, crabmeat and sweetcorn, reduce the heat to low and simmer, stirring frequently, until the gumbo thickens, about 10 minutes. Remove and discard the bay leaf.

✳ To serve, divide amongst 4 individual bowls.

Nutritional Analysis per Serving

Calories 277 (Kilojoules 1,163); Total fat 10g; Saturated fat 1g; Protein 26g; Cholesterol 68mg; Carbohydrates 22g; Sodium 660mg; Dietary fibre 6g; Calories from fat 32%

Turkey Vegetable Gumbo

125 g (4 oz) turkey sausages, cut
　　into 2.5 cm (1 inch) slices

1 onion, chopped

2 garlic cloves, very finely chopped

2 celery stalks, sliced

1 red pepper, seeded, cored and
　　chopped

2 teaspoons chilli powder

1 tablespoon chopped fresh thyme

1 tablespoon chopped fresh oregano

1 bay leaf

½ teaspoon salt

¼ teaspoon hot pepper sauce

375 g (12 oz) okra, sliced

3 large tomatoes, peeled, seeded
　　and diced

90 g (3 oz) uncooked pearl barley

750 ml (24 fl oz) Chicken Stock
　　(recipe on page 206) or canned
　　reduced sodium chicken broth

Storage Tip

✳ Store this soup in an airtight container
in the refrigerator for up to 3 days or in
the freezer for up to 3 months.

Preparation: 30 minutes ✳ *Cooking: 45 minutes* ✳ *Serves 4*

This thick soup is a good example of using animal protein – here, turkey sausage – as a flavouring element in a dish rather than as the centre of the meal. Sautéing the vegetables with the meat and then simmering them in the stock provides the desired spicy sausage taste, but each serving contains only 30 g (1 oz) of meat, which is well within healthy eating guidelines.

✳ Coat a large non-stick saucepan with non-stick cooking spray and place over a medium heat. Add the sausage and sauté until browned all over and no longer pink in the centre, about 5 minutes. Add the onion, garlic, celery and pepper. Sauté until the vegetables are tender, about 5 minutes.

✳ Add the chilli powder, thyme, oregano, bay leaf, salt, hot pepper sauce, okra, tomatoes, barley and stock or broth and bring to the boil. Reduce the heat to low and simmer, stirring frequently, until the gumbo thickens and the barley is tender, about 30 minutes. Remove and discard the bay leaf.

✳ To serve, divide amongst 4 individual bowls.

Nutritional Analysis per Serving

Calories 197 (Kilojoules 827); Total fat 4g; Saturated fat 1g; Protein 15g; Cholesterol 22mg; Carbohydrates 28g; Sodium 540mg; Dietary fibre 6g; Calories from fat 18%

Hearty Vegetable Stew

2 teaspoons olive oil

1 onion, chopped

½ head green cabbage
(about 250 g/8 oz), cut into
5 cm (2 in) pieces

2 carrots, cut into 2.5 cm (1 in)
pieces

2 celery stalks, cut into 2.5 cm
(1 in) pieces

1 courgette, cut into 2.5 cm (1 in)
pieces

4 small red potatoes about 500 g (1 lb),
unpeeled, cut into 2.5 cm
(1 in) pieces

250g (8 oz) fresh mushrooms, sliced

6 tomatoes, peeled, seeded and diced

440 ml (14 fl oz) Chicken Stock
(recipe on page 206) or canned
reduced sodium chicken broth

15 g (½ oz) fresh basil, chopped

1 tablespoon fresh thyme, chopped

½ teaspoon salt

¼ teaspoon ground black pepper

Preparation: 20 minutes ✳ Cooking: 45 minutes ✳ Serves 4

This combination of winter vegetables is a rich source of anti-oxidants, getting vitamin C from cabbage and tomatoes and beta-carotene from the carrots. It makes a perfect choice for a packed lunch. If you have facilities for reheating, just pack portions in an airtight container. If not, invest in a wide-mouth vacuum bottle, and you can look forward to your healthy lunch all morning long. Use the time you save by not going out for lunch to take a brisk walk.

✳ In a large saucepan over a medium heat, heat the oil. Add the onion and cabbage and sauté until tender, about 5 minutes. Add the carrots, celery, courgette, potatoes and mushrooms and sauté for 5 minutes.

✳ Add the tomatoes, stock or broth, basil, thyme, salt and pepper. Bring to the boil, then reduce the heat to low and simmer until the potatoes are tender, about 30 minutes.

✳ To serve, divide amongst 4 individual bowls.

Nutritional Analysis per Serving

Calories 186 (Kilojoules 781); Total fat 4g; Saturated fat 0g; Protein 7g; Cholesterol 0mg; Carbohydrates 31g; Sodium 400mg; Dietary fibre 7g; Calories from fat 19%

Chicken Soup with Parsley Dumplings

*Preparation: 30 minutes * Cooking: 20 minutes * Serves 4*

Carrots, green beans and fresh herbs give this chicken noodle soup colour and flavour; the parsley dumplings make it a meal in a bowl. If you have it available, substitute 375 g (12 oz) of cooked chicken for the breast.

375 g (12 oz) skinless, boneless chicken breast

875 ml (28 fl oz) Chicken Stock (recipe on page 206) or canned reduced sodium chicken broth

375 ml (12 fl oz) water

2 bay leaves

1 tablespoon chopped fresh thyme

1 teaspoon chopped fresh sage

¼ teaspoon ground black pepper

½ teaspoon salt

1 onion, chopped

2 carrots, cut into 1 cm (1½ in) thick slices

250 g (8 oz) green beans, trimmed

125 g (4 oz) dried egg noodles

75 g (2½ oz) unbleached plain flour

2 tablespoons chopped fresh flat leaf parsley

¾ teaspoon baking powder

⅛ teaspoon bicarbonate of soda

⅛ teaspoon ground white pepper

1½ teaspoons margarine

60 ml (2 fl oz) buttermilk

1 egg white

* To make the soup, in a medium saucepan over a medium-high heat, poach the chicken breast in 2.5 cm (1 in) of water until it is no longer pink in the centre, about 10 minutes. Transfer to a work surface and cut into bite-sized pieces.

* In a large saucepan over a medium heat, combine the stock or broth, water, bay leaves, thyme, sage, black pepper and half the salt and bring to the boil. Add the onion, carrots, green beans, noodles and cooked chicken. Return to the boil, then reduce the heat to low and simmer until the carrots are tender, about 3 minutes.

* To make the dumplings, in a large bowl, combine the flour, parsley, baking powder, bicarbonate of soda, remaining salt and white pepper. Add the margarine and, using a fork, stir until the mixture resembles coarse crumbs. In a small bowl, combine the buttermilk and egg white and whisk until blended. Add to the flour mixture and stir until just blended.

* Divide the dough into 4 pieces and gently place on top of the soup. Simmer, covered, until the dumplings are puffed up, 10–12 minutes. Remove and discard the bay leaves.

* To serve, place one dumpling in each of 4 bowls and top each with an equal amount of the soup.

Cooking Tip

* Make the dumplings just before placing them on the hot soup to prevent the baking powder rising too soon.

Nutritional Analysis per Serving

Calories 362 (Kilojoules 1,520); Total fat 8g; Saturated fat 1g; Protein 33g; Cholesterol 75mg; Carbohydrates 44g; Sodium 743mg; Dietary fibre 4g; Calories from fat 20%

440 g (14 oz) dried black beans

2 litres (3½ pints) water

2 litres (3½ pints) Vegetable
    Stock (recipe on page 207)

1 large onion, chopped

2 garlic cloves, very finely chopped

2 carrots, sliced in 1 cm (½ inch)
    pieces

1½ teaspoons ground cumin

1 teaspoon chilli powder

60 ml (2 fl oz) orange juice

10 g (⅓ oz) fresh coriander, chopped

60 ml (2 fl oz) soured cream

Cooking Tip

✽ You may find it easiest simply to soak the beans overnight in water to cover, drain them and begin making the soup at the second step. If you prefer a smooth texture, purée all the soup in the fourth step.

Black Bean Soup

Preparation: 20 minutes ✽ Cooking: 2½ hours ✽ Serves 4

This filling, flavourful soup is completely vegetarian and very low in fat, but I have to admit a preference for a delicious meat version. I add 125 g (4 oz) chopped chorizo, a cooked pork sausage, along with the onion. The nutritional analysis of that version: calories 583 (kilojoules 2,450), total fat 12g, saturated fat 3g, protein 32g, cholesterol 24mg, carbohydrates 89g, sodium 558mg, dietary fibre 15g, and calories from fat 18%.

✽ In a large pot over a high heat, combine the beans and water and bring to the boil. Reduce the heat to medium and cook for 10 minutes, skimming away the grey foam that appears. Drain well.

✽ In a large saucepan over a medium heat, combine the beans and stock and bring to the boil. Reduce the heat to low and simmer for 1½ hours.

✽ Coat a large non-stick frying pan with non-stick cooking spray and place over a medium heat. Add the onion and garlic and sauté until the onion is tender, about 5 minutes. Stir the onion mixture into the beans. Add the carrots, cumin, chilli powder and orange juice. Simmer for 45 minutes.

✽ Remove 250 g (8 oz) of the mixture, place in a food processor with the metal blade or in a blender, purée until smooth and return to the pot. Remove from the heat and stir in half the coriander.

✽ To serve, divide amongst 4 individual bowls. Top each with an equal amount of the soured cream and remaining coriander.

Nutritional Analysis per Serving

Calories 411 (Kilojoules 1,726); Total fat 5g; Saturated fat 2.5g; Protein 27g; Cholesterol 9mg; Carbohydrates 66g; Sodium 42mg; Dietary fibre 10g; Calories from fat 12%

Pasta and Watercress Soup

2 teaspoons olive oil

2 leeks, green and white parts,
  finely chopped

2 carrots, peeled and chopped

1.5 litres (2½ pints) Vegetable
  Stock (recipe on page 207)

10 g (⅓ oz) fresh thyme, chopped

2 tablespoons chopped fresh oregano

250 g (8 oz) dried elbow pasta

250 g (8 oz) watercress, stalks removed

¼ teaspoon ground black pepper

Cooking Tip

✳ To chop fresh herbs, rinse them under
cold running water and dry thoroughly
by shaking or gently patting with tea
towels. If leaves are attached to woody
stalks, pull them off. Gather the leaves
into a compact bunch and, with a sharp
knife, carefully cut crossways to chop
coarsely. Chop further if a finer consistency
is required.

Preparation: 20 minutes ✳ Cooking: 45 minutes ✳ Serves 4

*Peppery-tasting watercress, a member of the mustard family that packs
a good amount of vitamin C, has small, dark green leaves on a stalk
slightly thicker than that of parsley. It's usually available commercially
all year. If you're growing it in your herb garden, water it generously
and expect peak supplies in late spring.*

✳ In a large saucepan over a medium heat, heat the oil. Add the
leeks and carrots and sauté, stirring frequently, until tender, about
10 minutes.

✳ Add the stock, thyme and oregano, increase the heat to
medium-high and bring to the boil.

✳ Reduce the heat to low, cover and simmer for 20 minutes.

✳ Uncover, increase the heat to medium-high and bring to the
boil. Add the pasta and watercress and cook according to the
packet instructions or until the pasta is al dente, about 10 minutes.
Add the pepper.

✳ To serve, divide amongst 4 individual bowls.

Nutritional Analysis per Serving

Calories 343 (Kilojoules 1,440); Total fat 4g; Saturated fat 1g; Protein 10g;
Cholesterol 0mg; Carbohydrates 52g; Sodium 136mg; Dietary fibre 5g;
Calories from fat 10%

1 teaspoon margarine

1 large onion, chopped

2 celery stalks, chopped

1.2 litres (2 pints) Chicken Stock
(recipe on page 206) or canned
reduced sodium chicken broth

750 g (1½ lb) potatoes, cut into
2.5 cm (1 in) cubes

10 g (⅓ oz) fresh parsley, chopped

30 g (1 oz) reduced fat Cheddar
cheese, grated

¼ teaspoon ground white pepper

4 fresh flat-leaf parsley sprigs

Shopping Tip

✳ If fresh herbs are not available, substitute dried herbs, which have a stronger flavour. Use a ratio of 1:4, that is, about one-fourth of the amount of dried herbs to the fresh herbs called for in a recipe.

Potato Soup

Preparation: 25 minutes ✳ Cooking: 55 minutes ✳ Serves 4

Leaving the potato skins intact adds extra texture, vitamins and fibre to this puréed soup, which has the look of a traditional cream soup but only a fraction of the fat of dairy products.

✳ In a large saucepan over a medium heat, melt the margarine. Add the onion and celery and sauté, stirring frequently, until tender, about 10 minutes.

✳ Add the stock or broth and potatoes, increase the heat to medium-high and bring to the boil.

✳ Reduce the heat to low, cover and simmer until the potatoes are tender when pierced with a fork, about 30 minutes.

✳ Remove from the heat, add the chopped parsley, stir to mix well and let stand for 5 minutes.

✳ Strain the soup, reserving the liquid, and transfer the vegetables to a food processor with the metal blade or to a blender. Add 250 ml (8 fl oz) of the reserved liquid to the vegetable mixture and process until smooth.

✳ In the same saucepan over a medium-low heat, combine the purée, remaining reserved liquid, cheese and pepper. Simmer, stirring frequently, until the cheese melts, about 5 minutes.

✳ To serve, divide amongst 4 individual bowls. Top each with a parsley sprig.

Nutritional Analysis per Serving

Calories 205 (Kilojoules 861); Total fat 4g; Saturated fat 1g; Protein 10g; Cholesterol 3mg; Carbohydrates 34g; Sodium 359mg; Dietary fibre 3g; Calories from fat 17%

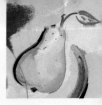

500 g (1 lb) skinless, boneless chicken
  breasts, cut into thin strips

3 garlic cloves, very finely chopped

250 g (8 oz) canned tomato
  purée

60 ml (2 fl oz) dark molasses

2 tablespoons Dijon mustard

2 tablespoons white wine vinegar

1 teaspoon chilli powder

¼ teaspoon salt

¼ teaspoon hot pepper sauce

4 wholewheat rolls, halved and toasted

Storage Tip

✳ The shredded chicken with its spicy
sauce can be stored in an airtight container in the refrigerator for up to 4 days.

Shredded Chicken Sandwich

Preparation: 10 minutes ✳ *Cooking: 20 minutes* ✳ *Serves 4*

*In just 30 minutes, you can enjoy the flavours of slow-cooked Southern
barbecue — tomatoes, molasses, mustard, vinegar, chilli powder and hot
pepper sauce — in this deliciously healthy, traditionally messy sandwich.*

✳ Coat a large non-stick frying pan with non-stick cooking
spray and place over a medium heat. Add the chicken and sauté
until it is no longer pink in the centre, about 5 minutes.

✳ To make the sauce, in a medium bowl, combine the garlic,
tomato purée, molasses, mustard, vinegar, chilli powder, salt and
hot pepper sauce and whisk until blended.

✳ When the chicken is cooked, add the sauce, bring to the boil,
reduce the heat to low and simmer until the liquid is reduced by
half and the chicken is tender, about 10 minutes. Using a slotted
spoon, transfer the chicken to a work surface. Using 2 forks, pull
the chicken into thin shreds and return it to the sauce.

✳ To serve, place one half of each bun on 4 individual plates.
Top each with an equal amount of the chicken, sauce and the
other half of the bun.

Nutritional Analysis per Serving

Calories 340 (Kilojoules 1,439); Total fat 3g; Saturated fat 1g; Protein 38g;
Cholesterol 88mg; Carbohydrates 43g; Sodium 884mg; Dietary fibre 5g;
Calories from fat 8%

500 g (1 lb) minced skinless chicken
   breast
45 g (1½ oz) spring onions, green and
   white parts, chopped
30 g (1 oz) dried breadcrumbs
2 teaspoons Worcestershire sauce
½ teaspoon hot pepper sauce
¼ teaspoon salt
1 egg white
4 wholemeal hamburger buns,
   halved and lightly toasted
4 lettuce leaves

Creamy Horseradish

125 ml (4 fl oz) soured cream
60 g (2 oz) horseradish, drained
   and grated
2 tablespoons white wine vinegar
¼ teaspoon ground black pepper

Shopping Tip

* You can easily mince your own meat by
purchasing skinless, boneless chicken
breasts, cutting them into chunks and
chopping them in a food processor with a
metal blade.

Spicy Chicken Burgers
with Creamy Horseradish

*Preparation: 15 minutes * Cooking: 10 minutes * Serves 4*

*Hot sauce, spring onions and a horseradish dressing spice up the flavour
of these healthy burgers. Make the Creamy Horseradish before you cook
your burgers.*

* In a bowl, combine the chicken, spring onions, breadcrumbs,
Worcestershire sauce, hot pepper sauce, salt and egg white. Stir to
mix well. Transfer to a work surface, divide into 4 equal
portions and shape each portion into a patty 2.5 cm
(1 in) thick.

* Coat a large non-stick frying pan with non-stick cooking
spray. Place the frying pan over a medium heat, add the patties
and cook, covered, until browned, about 5 minutes. Turn and
cook, covered, until the chicken is no longer pink in the centre,
about 5 minutes.

* To serve, spread 1 tablespoon of the Creamy Horseradish on
each half bun. Place one half of each bun on 4 individual plates.
Top each with a lettuce leaf, a burger and the other half of the bun.

Creamy Horseradish

* In a small bowl, combine the soured cream, horseradish,
vinegar and pepper and whisk until blended.

* Store in an airtight container in the refrigerator for up to
3 days. One serving is 2 tablespoons.

Nutritional Analysis per Serving

Calories 366 (Kilojoules 1,543); Total fat 10g; Saturated fat 6g; Protein 38g;
Cholesterol 110mg; Carbohydrates 32g; Sodium 517mg; Dietary fibre 4g;
Calories from fat 25%

Turkey Burgers with Mushroom Sauce

500 g (1 lb) minced turkey breast

1 small onion, chopped

30 g (1 oz) dried breadcrumbs

1 egg white

¼ teaspoon salt

¼ teaspoon mustard powder

½ teaspoon ground black pepper

125 g (4 oz) fresh mushrooms, sliced

125 ml (4 fl oz) Chicken Stock
   (recipe on page 206) or canned
   reduced sodium chicken broth

1 tablespoon chopped fresh thyme

125 ml (4 fl oz) soured cream

4 sesame seed hamburger buns, halved

Preparation: 15 minutes ✳ *Cooking: 15 minutes* ✳ *Serves 4*

Readily available ground turkey breast has a robust flavour and is a low fat alternative to ground beef. You can also mince your own turkey breast using a food processor.

✳ In a large bowl, combine the turkey, onion, breadcrumbs, egg white, salt, mustard and ¼ teaspoon of the pepper and toss to mix well. Transfer to a work surface, divide into 4 equal portions and shape each portion into a patty 2.5 cm (1 in) thick.

✳ Coat a large non-stick frying pan with non-stick cooking spray. Place the frying pan over a medium heat, add the patties and cook, covered, until browned, about 5 minutes. Turn and cook, covered, until the turkey is no longer pink in the centre, about 5 minutes.

✳ To make the mushroom sauce, coat a small non-stick frying pan with non-stick cooking spray. Place the frying pan over a medium heat, add the mushrooms and sauté until they are tender and release their juices, about 3 minutes. Add the stock or broth and thyme and bring to the boil, then reduce the heat to low and simmer for 5 minutes. Add the soured cream and remaining ¼ teaspoon pepper and simmer until the sauce thickens, about 2 minutes.

✳ To serve, place one half of each bun on 4 individual plates. Top with a burger, an equal amount of the mushroom sauce and the other half of the bun.

Nutritional Analysis per Serving

Calories 357 (Kilojoules 1,504); Total fat 9g; Saturated fat 5g; Protein 38g; Cholesterol 90mg; Carbohydrates 32g; Sodium 503mg; Dietary fibre 1g; Calories from fat 24%

375 g (12 oz) water-packed tuna,
   drained
1 red pepper, seeded, cored and diced
125 g (4 oz) virtually no fat
   plain yogurt
2 tablespoons chopped fresh flat-leaf
   parsley
1 tablespoon Dijon mustard
1 tablespoon red wine vinegar
¼ teaspoon ground black pepper
90 g (3 oz) rocket, stalks trimmed
2 wholemeal pitta breads, 20 cm
   (8 in) in diameter, halved

Nutrition Tip

✳ Check those tuna cans carefully before
purchase. The nutritional differences
between oil-packed chunk light tuna and
water-packed solid white are remarkable.
Per 100 g (3½ oz) serving, oil-packed
contains 189 calories, 9 g fat, 5 g saturated
fat and 27.1 g protein. In comparison, the
same amount of water-packed contains
just 99 calories, 0.6 g fat and 0.2 g
saturated fat, as well as 23.5 g protein.

Tuna Salad Sandwich

Preparation: 25 minutes ✳ Serves 4

*The combination of tangy yogurt and mustard, peppery rocket and
vitamin C-rich red pepper makes for a refreshing change of pace from
everyday tuna sandwiches.*

✳ In a large bowl, combine the tuna and pepper and toss to
mix well. Add the yogurt, parsley, mustard, vinegar and pepper
and stir until blended.

✳ To serve, place an equal amount of the tuna mixture and rocket
into each pitta half. One serving is a half pitta.

Nutritional Analysis per Serving

Calories 233 (Kilojoules 991); Total fat 2g; Saturated fat 0.5g; Protein 28g;
Cholesterol 49mg; Carbohydrates 28g; Sodium 612mg; Dietary fibre 3g;
Calories from fat 7.2%

Tomato-Basil Pizza

Preparation: 25 minutes ✳ *Cooking: 20 minutes* ✳ *Serves 4*

Tomatoes and basil are a traditional Mediterranean flavour combination that is well represented in this quick pizza. In the summer, try using different types of fresh tomatoes, including red or yellow cherry tomatoes. When pressed for time, spread the sauce on commercial pizza bread shells and bake as instructed on the packet.

30 sun-dried tomatoes, packed
   without oil

500 g (1 lb) plum tomatoes,
   peeled, seeded and diced

125 ml (4 fl oz) Chicken Stock
   (recipe on page 206) or canned
   reduced sodium chicken broth

15 g (½ oz) firmly packed
   fresh basil leaves

2 garlic cloves, very finely chopped

3 tablespoons grated pecorino cheese

¼ teaspoon salt

¼ teaspoon ground black pepper

1 teaspoon olive oil

500 g (1 lb) Karen's Pizza Dough
   (recipe on page 185)

2 tablespoons pine nuts, lightly toasted

✳ Preheat the oven to 230°C (450°F/Gas 8). Coat 2 large baking sheets with non-stick cooking spray.

✳ In a small saucepan over a medium heat, combine the sun-dried tomatoes, fresh tomatoes and stock or broth. Bring to the boil, then reduce the heat to low and simmer until the sun-dried tomatoes are tender, about 5 minutes.

✳ In a food processor with the metal blade or in a blender, combine the basil, garlic, pecorino cheese, salt and pepper. Process until smooth. With the motor running, gradually add the olive oil and process until blended. Add the tomato mixture to the basil mixture and pulse on and off until just blended.

✳ Divide the pizza dough into 4 equal portions. On a lightly floured work surface, roll out each portion into an 20 cm (8 in) round. Place on the prepared sheets and form a 1 cm (½ in) raised lip round the edges. Top each round with an equal amount of the tomato and basil mixture and pine nuts, leaving a 1 cm (½ in) border around the edges.

✳ Bake until the crusts are golden, about 15 minutes.

✳ To serve, place on 4 individual plates.

Cooking Tip

✳ To peel fresh tomatoes, bring a saucepan of water to the boil. With a small, sharp knife, cut out the core at the stalk end of each tomato and score a shallow X in the skin at the opposite end. One at a time and using a slotted spoon, immerse the tomatoes in the boiling water for about 10 seconds to loosen their skins. Lift out and dip in a bowl of cold water to cool. Then, starting at the X, peel off the skin, using the knife blade to help you if necessary.

Nutritional Analysis per Serving

Calories 563 (Kilojoules 2,377); Total fat 17g; Saturated fat 3g; Protein 20g; Cholesterol 8mg; Carbohydrates 89g; Sodium 723mg; Dietary fibre 8g; Calories from fat 27%

15 g (½ oz) dried porcini
   mushrooms, stalks removed
15 g (½ oz) dried shiitake
   mushrooms, stalks removed
250 ml (8 fl oz) Chicken Stock
   (recipe on page 206) or canned
   reduced sodium chicken broth
2 tablespoons chopped fresh thyme
¼ teaspoon ground black pepper
500 g (1 lb) Karen's Pizza Dough
   (recipe on page 185)
2 teaspoons extra virgin olive oil
30 g (1 oz) pecorino cheese, grated
2 tablespoons chopped fresh flat-leaf
   parsley

Shopping Tip

✷ Well-stocked markets carry both of
these dried mushrooms. You may also find
porcini mushrooms in Italian delicatessens
and shiitake mushrooms in Asian markets.

Mushroom-Cheese Pizza

Preparation: 25 minutes ✳ *Cooking: 25 minutes* ✳ *Serves 4*

*Two types of dried mushrooms give a wonderful, earthy flavour to this
foccacia-style pizza – that is, a pizza without sauce as a topping. Unlike
many pizzas, which are just as good hot or cold, this one is best eaten
soon after baking as it tends to dry out as it cools.*

✳ Preheat the oven to 230°C (450°F/Gas 8). Coat a large baking
sheet with non-stick cooking spray.

✳ In a saucepan over a medium heat, combine the mushrooms,
stock or broth and thyme. Bring to the boil, then reduce the heat
to low and simmer until the liquid is absorbed, about 15 minutes.
Add the pepper and stir to mix well. Cool the mushrooms in the
pan, then transfer to a work surface and slice into thin strips.

✳ On a lightly floured work surface, roll out the pizza dough
into a 30 cm (12 in) round. Place on the prepared sheet and
form a 1 cm (½ in) raised lip round the edge. Brush the olive oil
over the dough. Top with the mushrooms and pecorino cheese,
leaving a 1 cm (½ in) border round the edge.

✳ Bake until the crust is golden, about 15 minutes.

✳ To serve, top the pizza with the parsley. Slice into quarters
and place on 4 individual plates.

Nutritional Analysis per Serving

Calories 510 (Kilojoules 2,155); Total fat 13g; Saturated fat 3g; Protein 19g;
Cholesterol 8mg; Carbohydrates 85g; Sodium 589mg; Dietary fibre 8g;
Calories from fat 23%

1 onion, chopped

2 garlic cloves, very finely chopped

250 g (8 oz) minced bison or lean
    minced beef

1 tablespoon herbes de Provence

250 g (8 oz) fresh mushrooms, sliced

1 kg (2¼ lb) plum tomatoes,
    peeled, seeded and diced

1 teaspoon salt

½ teaspoon ground black pepper

30 g cup (1 oz) Parmesan
    cheese, grated

500 g (1 lb) Karen's Pizza Dough
    (recipe on page 185)

125 g (4 oz) mozzarella
    cheese, shredded

Cooking Tip

✱ Herbes de Provence are a blend of
dried herbs typical of Provence, France.
To make your own, combine ½ teaspoon
each of thyme, rosemary, sage, marjoram,
basil, fennel seed and mint.

Ted's Favourite Pizza

Preparation: 25 minutes ✱ *Cooking: 25 minutes* ✱ *Serves 4*

Ted enjoys this pizza because it features bison, which we raise on our ranch in Montana. The metabolism of bison is such that fat is not deposited within the muscles, resulting in a much leaner red meat than beef. Because of its health benefits and great taste, bison meat is growing in popularity.

✱ Preheat the oven to 220°C (425°F/Gas 7). Coat a large baking sheet with non-stick cooking spray.

✱ Coat a large non-stick frying pan with non-stick cooking spray. Place over a medium heat, add the onion and garlic and sauté for 2 minutes. Add the bison or beef and herbs and sauté until the meat is no longer pink, about 5 minutes for bison and 7 minutes for beef. Add the mushrooms, tomatoes, salt and pepper and simmer until the liquid evaporates, about 10 minutes. Remove from the heat and stir in the Parmesan cheese.

✱ On a lightly floured work surface, roll out the pizza dough into a 30 cm (12 in) round. Place on the prepared sheet and form a 1 cm (½ in) raised lip round the edge. Top with the meat mixture and the mozzarella, leaving a 1 cm (½ in) border round the edge.

✱ Bake until the crust is golden and the cheese is bubbly, about 15 minutes.

✱ To serve, slice into quarters and place on 4 individual plates.

Nutritional Analysis per Serving

Calories 825 (Kilojoules 3,477); Total fat 31g; Saturated fat 14g;
Protein 5og; Cholesterol 83mg; Carbohydrates 93g; Sodium 1,538mg;
Dietary fibre 10g; Calories from fat 33%

1 teaspoon plus 1 tablespoon olive oil

2 garlic cloves, very finely chopped

2 tablespoons chopped fresh oregano

½ teaspoon salt

½ teaspoon ground black pepper

375 g (12 oz) lean beef fillet, trimmed of visible fat and cut into 2.5 cm (1 in) chunks

1 cucumber (about 375 g/12 oz), seeded and chopped

2 plum tomatoes (185 g/6 oz), sliced

1 small red onion, thinly sliced

30 g (1 oz) feta cheese, crumbled

10 g (⅓ oz) fresh flat-leaf parsley, chopped

4 Kalamata olives, stoned

2 tablespoons lemon juice

1 teaspoon finely grated lemon rind

Cooking Tip

✳ To stone an olive, use an olive stoner, which grips the olive and pushes out the stone. Or, using a small, sharp knife, slit the olive lengthways down to the stone and pry away the flesh.

Greek Salad

Preparation: 20 minutes ✳ *Cooking: 5 minutes* ✳ *Serves 4*

In addition to the preparation time, the beef must marinate for 1 hour. While you can use any type of olive in this dish, Kalamata olives provide the authentic taste of Greece, evoking warm days spent on island beaches. For this reason, the salad is ideal to serve when lunching outdoors.

✳ In a non-metallic dish, combine the 1 teaspoon olive oil and half the garlic, oregano, salt and pepper and stir to mix well. Add the beef and toss to coat. Cover and refrigerate to marinate for 1 hour.

✳ Coat a frying pan with non-stick cooking spray and place over a medium-high heat. Using a slotted spoon, transfer the beef to the pan, reserving the marinade, and cook, stirring frequently, for 3 minutes. Add the marinade to the pan and cook until the beef is no longer pink in the centre, about 2 minutes more.

✳ Using a slotted spoon, transfer the beef to a large bowl. Discard the marinade. To the bowl, add the cucumber, tomatoes, onion, cheese, parsley and olives.

✳ In a small bowl, combine the 1 tablespoon olive oil, garlic, oregano, salt and pepper and the lemon juice and lemon rind, and whisk until blended. Add to the vegetable mixture and toss to coat well.

✳ To serve, divide amongst 4 individual plates.

Nutritional Analysis per Serving

Calories 245 (Kilojoules 1,020); Total fat 15g; Saturated fat 5.5g; Protein 23g; Cholesterol 58mg; Carbohydrates 5g; Sodium 519mg; Dietary fibre 1.5g; Calories from fat 55%

8 corn tortillas, 20 cm (8 in)
in diameter
375 g (12 oz) cos lettuce, chopped
3 plum tomatoes, seeded
and chopped
1 spring onion, green and
white parts, chopped
30 g (1 oz) reduced fat
Cheddar cheese, grated

Avocado Dressing

1 avocado, peeled, seeded and mashed
125 ml (4 fl oz) soured cream
2 tablespoons lime juice
1 garlic clove, very finely chopped
½ teaspoon chilli powder

Storage Tip

* The Avocado Dressing can be stored
in an airtight container in the refrigerator
for up to 4 days.

Taco Salad with Avocado Dressing

*Preparation: 25 minutes * Cooking: 15 minutes * Serves 4*

Avocados are a wonderful fruit but they do contain fat and should be used sparingly. This recipe uses just 1 avocado for 4 servings, which will not detrimentally affect your nutritional goals. Seek out Hass avocados with thick dark pebbly skins as they are considered to have the best flavour and texture. Make sure the avocado is absolutely ripe for optimum taste. For a healthy snack, skip the salad and serve the home-made corn chips with the dressing as a dip.

* Preheat the oven to 220°C (425°F/Gas 7).
* To make the corn chips, place the tortillas on ungreased baking sheets and bake until crisp, about 15 minutes, turning halfway through the cooking time. Cool to the touch and break into 5 cm (2 in) pieces.
* In a large bowl, combine the lettuce, tomatoes, green onion and cheese and toss to mix well.
* To serve, line 4 individual salad plates with an equal amount of the corn chips. Top each with an equal amount of the salad mixture and Avocado Dressing.

Avocado Dressing

* In a food processor with the metal blade or in a blender, combine the avocado, soured cream, lime juice, garlic and chilli powder. Process until smooth. One serving is 3 tablespoons.

Nutritional Analysis per Serving

Calories 323 (Kilojoules 1,356); Total fat 16g; Saturated fat 6g; Protein 9g;
Cholesterol 22mg; Carbohydrates 39g; Sodium 235mg; Dietary fibre 4g;
Calories from fat 44%

1.2 litres (2 pints) water

330 g (10½ oz) dried lentils, rinsed
and picked over

1 small red onion, chopped

1 tablespoon chopped fresh thyme

½ teaspoon ground allspice

60 ml (2 fl oz) red wine
vinegar

1 tablespoon Dijon mustard

1½ tablespoons olive oil

2 celery stalks, chopped

2 carrots, chopped

10 g (⅓ oz) fresh flat-leaf
parsley, chopped

1 teaspoon salt

¼ teaspoon ground black pepper

185 g (6 oz) smoked skinless turkey
breast, cut into bite-sized pieces

Lentil and Smoked Turkey Salad

Preparation: 20 minutes ✷ Cooking: 15 minutes ✷ Serves 4

Lentils, the disc-shaped seeds of a plant native to Asia, are an excellent source of non-fat protein in a healthy diet. Several different colours of lentils are available, and they are interchangeable for this cold salad. Smoked turkey is available in the delicatessen section of some supermarkets and from specialist smokers.

✷ In a medium saucepan over a medium-high heat, combine the water, lentils, onion, thyme and allspice. Bring to the boil, then reduce the heat to low and simmer until the lentils are tender but still intact, about 15 minutes.

✷ Drain the lentil mixture and transfer to a large bowl. Add the vinegar, mustard, olive oil, celery, carrots, parsley, salt and pepper. Refrigerate the salad for at least 15 minutes to allow the lentils and vegetables to marinate in the dressing, then bring to room temperature.

✷ To serve, divide amongst 4 individual plates. Top each with an equal amount of the turkey pieces.

Nutritional Analysis per Serving

Calories 397 (Kilojoules 1,679); Total fat 7g; Saturated fat 1g; Protein 36g; Cholesterol 38mg; Carbohydrates 51g; Sodium 672mg; Dietary fibre 5g; Calories from fat 15%

185 g (6 oz) bulgar

1 tablespoon chopped fresh oregano

1 teaspoon ground cumin

¼ teaspoon salt

¼ teaspoon ground black pepper

250 ml (8 fl oz) Chicken Stock (recipe on page 206) or canned reduced sodium chicken broth

250 ml (8 fl oz) water

3 tablespoons lemon juice

3 tablespoons olive oil

2 tablespoons virtually no fat plain yogurt

2 garlic cloves, very finely chopped

4 spring onions, green and white parts, chopped

1 teaspoon finely grated lemon rind

1 cucumber (about 375 g/12 oz), seeded and chopped

3 large tomatoes, seeded and chopped

10 g (⅓ oz) fresh flat-leaf (Italian) parsley, chopped

10 g (⅓ oz) chopped fresh mint

fresh flat-leaf parsley sprigs

Tabbouleh

Preparation: 20 minutes ✳ *Cooking: 20 minutes* ✳ *Serves 4*

At once robust, aromatic and refreshing, this salad is a classic of the Middle East. Bulgar, also known as cracked wheat, is flavourful and chewy and an excellent source of fibre. For variety, substitute other whole grains such as quinoa or barley.

✳ In a large bowl, combine the bulgar, oregano, cumin, salt and pepper and stir to mix well.

✳ In a small saucepan over medium-high heat, combine the stock or broth and the water and bring to the boil. Pour the boiling liquid over the bulgar mixture. Let stand until the liquid is absorbed, about 20 minutes.

✳ To make the dressing, in a small bowl, combine the lemon juice, olive oil, yogurt, garlic, spring onions and lemon rind and whisk until blended.

✳ To the bulgar mixture, add the dressing, cucumber, tomatoes, chopped parsley and mint and toss to coat well.

✳ To serve, divide amongst 4 individual plates. Garnish with the parsley sprigs.

Nutritional Analysis per Serving

Calories 278 (Kilojoules 1,157); Total fat 10g; Saturated fat 1g; Protein 7g; Cholesterol 0mg; Carbohydrates 41g; Sodium 161mg; Dietary fibre 10g; Calories from fat 31%

3 tablespoons crumbled goat's cheese

2 tablespoons soured cream

2 tablespoons skimmed milk

2 tablespoons snipped fresh chives

⅛ teaspoon ground black pepper

250 g (8 oz) mixed salad greens

3 tomatoes, seeded and sliced

1 red pepper, roasted, peeled, seeded,
   cored and cut into strips

Cooking Tip

✳ To roast a pepper, whether a sweet
pepper or a hot chilli pepper, cut the
pepper in half. Place on a baking sheet
under the grill or hold over a gas flame,
turning often, until blackened, about
5 minutes. Transfer to a paper bag, close
and set aside to cool, about 15 minutes.
Using a small knife, remove the skin,

Greens and Peppers Salad

Preparation: 15 minutes ✳ *Serves 4*

*Simple salad greens pack a lot of nutrition in fat-free, high-fibre form.
Chicory is rich in the B-vitamin folate and vitamins A and C, as well
as containing good amounts of calcium and potassium. Curly endive
offers folate and the anti-oxidant beta-carotene. Lamb's lettuce is very
rich in vitamins A and C. More common lettuces contain varying
but significant amounts of folate and vitamins A and C, with cos the
richest source. Many well-stocked markets amd greengrocers today
sell mixed greens already trimmed, washed and bagged, ready to toss
into a salad bowl.*

✳ To make the dressing, in a small bowl, combine the goat's
cheese, soured cream, milk, chives and pepper and whisk until
blended. The dressing can be stored in an airtight container for
up to 1 week.

✳ To serve, divide the greens amongst 4 individual plates.
Top each serving with an equal amount of the tomatoes, pepper
and dressing.

Nutritional Analysis per Serving

Calories 99 (Kilojoules 416); Total fat 5g; Saturated fat 3g; Protein 5g;
Cholesterol 14mg; Carbohydrates 9g; Sodium 222mg; Dietary fibre 2g;
Calories from fat 47%

Dinner

Suggested Dinner Menus

Most of us are used to eating our biggest meal in the evening. However, the hours before we go to sleep are not necessarily the best time to eat large quantities of food. The menus shown here and the recipes on the following pages creatively address both these factors. They offer robust satisfaction through complex carbohydrates that fill us up while being low in fat, easy to digest and calming to the nervous system. The recipes also include protein in reduced portions and are so imaginatively seasoned, cooked and presented that a little goes a long way – one of the wisest strategies in any healthy eating regimen.

Salmon with Sweetcorn Sauce
page 132

Spring Vegetable Sauté
page 197

*75 g (2½ oz)
steamed brown rice*

Summer Fruit in Rosemary Syrup
page 40

Nutritional Analysis per Serving: Calories 626 (Kilojoules 2,639); Total fat 17g; Saturated fat 3g; Protein 35g; Cholesterol 63mg; Carbohydrates 88g; Sodium 460mg; Dietary fibre 9g; Calories from fat 24%

Red Snapper Puttanesca
page 135

75 g (2½ oz) cooked wild rice

*75 g (2½ oz)
steamed courgettes*

Orange Pecan Drop Biscuits
page 216

Nutritional Analysis per Serving: Calories 460 (Kilojoules 1,944); Total fat 12g; Saturated fat 2g; Protein 34g; Cholesterol 58mg; Carbohydrates 56g; Sodium 520mg; Dietary fibre 4g; Calories from fat 23%

*Trout with
Hazelnut Shallot Sauce*
page 136

Spicy Rice Pilaff
page 208

*½ sliced tomato
with Mustard Vinaigrette*
page 184

Cranberry Apple Sauce
page 212

Nutritional Analysis per Serving: Calories 802 (Kilojoules 3,377); Total fat 25g; Saturated fat 3g; Protein 38g; Cholesterol 85mg; Carbohydrates 107g; Sodium 936mg; Dietary fibre 8g; Calories from fat 28%

Blackened Catfish
page 139

Garlic Mashed Potatoes
page 205

30 g (1 oz) mixed greens
with ½ tomato and
Sesame Garlic Dressing
page 184

Apple Walnut Bread
page 56

Nutritional Analysis per Serving: Calories 678 (Kilojoules 2,749); Total fat 18g; Saturated fat 2g; Protein 36g; Cholesterol 89mg; Carbohydrates 100g; Sodium 749mg; Dietary fibre 8g; Calories from fat 24%

Sesame Chicken and Mangetouts
in Apricot Sauce
page 140

60 g (2 oz) angel hair pasta

30 g (1 oz) mixed greens
with Basil Dressing
page 183

Banana Cheesecake
page 235

Nutritional Analysis per Serving: Calories 640 (Kilojoules 2,701); Total fat 17g; Saturated fat 5g; Protein 44g; Cholesterol 132mg; Carbohydrates 79g; Sodium 463mg; Dietary fibre 6g; Calories from fat 24%

Curried Chicken Stew
page 143

75 g (2½ oz)
steamed brown rice

Lemon Blueberry Ice Milk
page 224

Nutritional Analysis per Serving: Calories 378 (Kilojoules 1,598); Total fat 6g; Saturated fat 1g; Protein 37g; Cholesterol 89mg; Carbohydrates 49g; Sodium 270mg; Dietary fibre 4g; Calories from fat 14%

Roast Turkey
page 144

Bread and Apple Dressing
page 211

½ baked sweet potato

Spinach and Roasted Chestnuts
page 194

Pumpkin Spice Bread
page 231

Nutritional Analysis per Serving: Calories 1,122 (Kilojoules 4,740); Total fat 27g; Saturated fat 6g; Protein 68g; Cholesterol 206mg; Carbohydrates 163g; Sodium 1,141mg; Dietary fibre 14g; Calories from fat 22%

Mexican Chicken Casserole
page 147

Sweetcorn Pudding
page 201

Almond Gelatine Squares in Fruit
page 39

Nutritional Analysis per Serving: Calories 1,214 (Kilojoules 5,130); Total fat 20g; Saturated fat 5g; Protein 69g; Cholesterol 108mg; Carbohydrates 198g; Sodium 1,305mg; Dietary fibre 7g; Calories from fat 15%

Roast Pheasant
page 148

Rice, Raisin and
Rosemary Dressing
page 211

30 g (1 oz) steamed broccoli

Pears with Chocolate Sauce
page 219

Nutritional Analysis per Serving: Calories 1,433 (Kilojoules 6,024); Total fat 52g; Saturated fat 17g; Protein 100g; Cholesterol 715mg; Carbohydrates 152g; Sodium 952mg; Dietary fibre 7g; Calories from fat 33%

Garlic Pork Chops with Black Mushrooms
page 151

75 g (2½ oz) steamed mangetouts

Wild Rice with Mixed Dried Fruit
page 208

Almond Biscotti
page 215

Nutritional Analysis per Serving: Calories 591 (Kilojoules 2,499); Total fat 13g; Saturated fat 1g; Protein 38g; Cholesterol 91mg; Carbohydrates 84g; Sodium 762mg; Dietary fibre 7g; Calories from fat 20%

Beef Fillet with Artichokes and Pearl Onions
page 152

Rosemary Roasted Potatoes
page 202

1 celery stalk with Chive Chutney Dip
page 186

Baked Apples
page 223

Nutritional Analysis per Serving: Calories 750 (Kilojoules 3,172); Total fat 25g; Saturated fat 5g; Protein 49g; Cholesterol 78mg; Carbohydrates 91g; Sodium 507mg; Dietary fibre 9g; Calories from fat 30%

Bison Osso Buco
page 155

75 g (2½ oz) steamed rice

1 corn on the cob

Melon and Blueberries in Sauce
page 220

Nutritional Analysis per Serving: Calories 701 (Kilojoules 2,963); Total fat 12g; Saturated fat 3g; Protein 61g; Cholesterol 210mg; Carbohydrates 91g; Sodium 794mg; Dietary fibre 4g; Calories from fat 15%

Grilled Bison with Rosemary Marinade
page 156

Grilled Summer Vegetables
page 197

Orzo with Shallots and Herbs
page 205

Iced Cocoa
page 179

Nutritional Analysis per Serving: Calories 631 (Kilojoules 2,668); Total fat 14g; Saturated fat 4g; Protein 48g; Cholesterol 5mg; Carbohydrates 85g; Sodium 640mg; Dietary fibre 4g; Calories from fat 20%

Spaghetti in Spicy Peanut Sauce
page 159

110 g (3½ oz) steamed spinach

1 sliced cucumber with Mustard Vinaigrette
page 184

Banana Bread
page 52

Nutritional Analysis per Serving: Calories 748 (Kilojoules 3,169); Total fat 11g; Saturated fat 1g; Protein 22g; Cholesterol 0mg; Carbohydrates 148g; Sodium 780mg; Dietary fibre 9g; Calories from fat 13%

Lemon Broccoli Risotto
page 160

Steamed Carrots with Dill
page 194

30 g (1 oz) mixed greens with Sesame-Garlic Dressing
page 184

Sponge Cake with Chocolate-Orange Icing
page 227

Nutritional Analysis per Serving: Calories 619 (Kilojoules 2,600); Total fat 16g; Saturated fat 5g; Protein 18g; Cholesterol 56mg; Carbohydrates 103g; Sodium 413mg; Dietary fibre 7g; Calories from fat 23%

*Linguine with Goat's Cheese,
Tomatoes and Onions*
page 163

*Cos lettuce
with Sesame-Garlic Dressing*
page 184

*Italian bread with
1 teaspoon margarine*

Raspberry Sherbet
page 224

Nutritional Analysis per Serving: Calories 691
(Kilojoules 2,931); Total fat 16g; Saturated fat 4g;
Protein 23g; Cholesterol 14mg; Carbohydrates 124g;
Sodium 554mg; Dietary fibre 9g; Calories from fat 21%

Vegetable Lasagna
page 164

*30 g (1 oz) each steamed
peas and carrots*

1 hard roll

Honey Mint Fruit Compôte
page 231

Nutritional Analysis per Serving: Calories 668
(Kilojoules 2,818); Total fat 21g; Saturated fat 11g;
Protein 36g; Cholesterol 61mg; Carbohydrates 91g;
Sodium 721mg; Dietary fibre 12g; Calories from fat 28%

Bison Lasagna
page 167

5 spears steamed asparagus

2 breadsticks

Meringue Topped Cantaloupe
page 228

Nutritional Analysis per Serving: Calories 832
(Kilojoules 3,502); Total fat 21g; Saturated fat 10g;
Protein 49g; Cholesterol 90mg; Carbohydrates 122g;
Sodium 521mg; Dietary fibre 10g; Calories from fat 23%

Penne with Garlic Tomato Sauce
page 168

*1 slice French bread
with 1 teaspoon margarine*

*Poached Fruit with
Cinnamon Yogurt Topping*
page 36

Nutritional Analysis per Serving: Calories 633
(Kilojoules 2,822); Total fat 7g; Saturated fat 1g;
Protein 22g; Cholesterol 7mg; Carbohydrates 129g;
Sodium 557mg; Dietary fibre 8g; Calories from fat 10%

Spinach Soufflé
page 171

Ratatouille
page 198

Chocolate Cheesecake
page 236

Nutritional Analysis per Serving: Calories 772
(Kilojoules 3,235); Total fat 38g; Saturated fat 16g;
Protein 38g; Cholesterol 70mg; Carbohydrates 73g;
Sodium 925mg; Dietary fibre 10g; Calories from fat 44%

*Black Bean Enchiladas
with Tomato Salsa*
page 172

75 g (2½ oz) steamed rice

2 carrots with Avocado Dressing
page 115

*Orange Custard
with Raspberry Sauce*
page 232

Nutritional Analysis per Serving: Calories 1104
(Kilojoules 4,363); Total fat 34g; Saturated fat 14g;
Protein 39g; Cholesterol 250mg; Carbohydrates 152g;
Sodium 906mg; Dietary fibre 16g; Calories from fat 28%

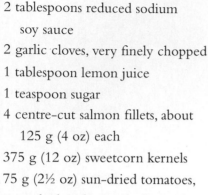

2 tablespoons reduced sodium
   soy sauce

2 garlic cloves, very finely chopped

1 tablespoon lemon juice

1 teaspoon sugar

4 centre-cut salmon fillets, about
   125 g (4 oz) each

375 g (12 oz) sweetcorn kernels

75 g (2½ oz) sun-dried tomatoes,
   packed without oil, chopped

125 ml (4 fl oz) water

½ teaspoon ground cumin

20 g (¾ oz) spring onions, green
   and white parts, chopped

10 g (⅓ oz) fresh coriander, chopped

1 teaspoon ground black pepper

Storage Tip

✻ The Sweetcorn Sauce, which is also
good on chicken breasts or halibut, can
be made ahead, refrigerated in an airtight
container for up to 2 days and reheated
in a small saucepan over a low heat while
the fish cooks.

Salmon with Sweetcorn Sauce

Preparation: 40 minutes ✻ *Cooking: 20 minutes* ✻ *Serves 4*

*When weather permits, cook the salmon on an outdoor charcoal grill for
a great summer dinner party. Although relatively high in fat as seafood
goes, salmon is a good source of omega-3 fatty acids, which benefit the
heart and circulatory system.*

✻ To make the marinade, in a shallow non-metallic dish, combine
the soy sauce, garlic, lemon juice and sugar. Add the salmon
fillets, turn to coat both sides, cover, refrigerate and marinate
for 15 minutes to 8 hours.

✻ To make the sauce, in a small saucepan over a medium–high
heat, combine the sweetcorn, tomatoes, water and cumin. Bring
to the boil, then reduce the heat to low and simmer until the
tomatoes are soft, about 10 minutes. Remove from the heat,
add the green onions and coriander and stir to mix well.

✻ In a large non-stick frying pan over a medium–high heat, heat
1 tablespoon of the marinade. Transfer the salmon to a work
surface and coat with the pepper. Discard the remaining marinade.

✻ Add the salmon to the hot pan and sauté for 4 minutes. Turn
and sauté the fish until it just separates when pressed with a fork,
about 4 minutes more.

✻ To serve, divide the fillets amongst 4 individual plates. Top
each with an equal amount of the sauce.

Nutritional Analysis per Serving

Calories 353 (Kilojoules 1,484); Total fat 15g; Saturated fat 3g; Protein 29g;
Cholesterol 63mg; Carbohydrates 28g; Sodium 312mg; Dietary fibre 1.5g;
Calories from fat 38%

Red Snapper Puttanesca

*Preparation: 25 minutes * Cooking: 40 minutes * Serves 4*

Puttanesca is a traditional Italian sauce made with capers, olives, anchovies and tomatoes. The rindy combination of flavours pairs perfectly with the delicate taste and texture of red snapper. The sauce can also be spooned over grilled chicken or pasta for a light, healthy meal in minutes. Make the sauce ahead and refrigerate in an airtight container for up to 3 days.

4 red snapper fillets, about 125 g
   (4 oz) each
1 tablespoon lemon juice
¼ teaspoon ground black pepper
2 teaspoons olive oil
1 onion, diced
3 garlic cloves, very finely chopped
3 large tomatoes, peeled and chopped
8 Niçoise olives, stoned and sliced
2 tablespoons drained capers
1 tablespoon finely chopped canned
   anchovies
10 g (⅓ oz) fresh basil, chopped
1 tablespoon chopped fresh oregano
1 bay leaf
10 g (⅓ oz) fresh flat-leaf parsley,
   chopped
½ lemon, cut into 4 wedges
4 fresh flat-leaf parsley sprigs

* Preheat the oven to 180°C (350°F/Gas 4).
* Place the snapper fillets in a shallow non-metallic dish and top with the lemon juice and pepper.
* To make the sauce, in a large non-stick frying pan over a medium heat, heat the oil. Add the onion and garlic and sauté, stirring frequently, for 2 minutes. Add the tomatoes, olives, capers, anchovies, basil, oregano and bay leaf. Bring to the boil, then reduce the heat to low and simmer for 5 minutes.
* Pour the sauce over the fillets and top with the chopped parsley. Cover with aluminium foil and bake until the fish just separates when pressed with a fork, about 30 minutes. Remove and discard the bay leaf.
* To serve, divide amongst 4 individual plates. Top each with a lemon wedge and a parsley sprig.

Nutrition Tip

* Although garlic does not provide any significant quantities of nutrients, some medical studies have found that it contains certain substances that can reduce elevated blood cholesterol levels.

Nutritional Analysis per Serving

Calories 166 (Kilojoules 701); Total fat 5g; Saturated fat 1g; Protein 26g;
Cholesterol 46mg; Carbohydrates 4g; Sodium 338mg; Dietary fibre 1g;
Calories from fat 27%

75 g (2½ oz) stone-ground yellow
cornmeal

75 g (2½ oz) wholemeal breadcrumbs

10 g (⅓ oz) fresh flat-leaf parsley,
chopped

1 tablespoon finely grated lemon rind

½ teaspoon ground black pepper

3 garlic cloves, very finely chopped

250 ml (8 fl oz) buttermilk

4 rainbow trout fillets, about 125 g
(4 oz) each

1 tablespoon hazelnut oil

2 small shallots, chopped

30g (1 oz) hazelnuts, chopped

60 ml (2 fl oz) Vegetable Stock (recipe
on page 207)

2 tablespoons lemon juice

½ lemon, cut into 4 wedges

4 fresh flat-leaf parsley sprigs

Nutrition Tip

✱ Serve with low fat accompaniments
(menu on page 128) to get a meal with
calories from fat below 25 per-cent.

Trout with Hazelnut Shallot Sauce

Preparation: 20 minutes ✱ *Cooking: 30 minutes* ✱ *Serves 4*

Trout, like salmon, is rich in beneficial omega-3 fatty acids. The cornmeal coating and hazelnut sauce provide good fibre as well as adding distinctive flavour and crunchy texture. The breading is equally good on skinless chicken and turkey breasts.

✱ Preheat the oven to 200°C (400°F/Gas 6). Coat a shallow non-metallic dish with non-stick cooking spray.

✱ In a large shallow dish, combine the cornmeal, breadcrumbs, chopped parsley, lemon rind, pepper and half of the garlic.

✱ Pour the buttermilk into another shallow dish. Add the trout and turn to coat both sides. Remove the fish from the buttermilk and place in the cornmeal mixture. Turn to coat both sides, pressing the mixture into the fish.

✱ Place the fish in the prepared dish and bake, uncovered, until it just separates when pressed with a fork, about 20 minutes.

✱ To make the sauce, in a medium non-stick frying pan over a medium heat, heat the oil. Add the shallots and the remaining garlic and sauté for 2 minutes. Add the hazelnuts and sauté for 2 minutes more. Add the stock and lemon juice and simmer for 5 minutes.

✱ To serve, divide amongst 4 individual plates. Top each with an equal amount of the sauce, a lemon wedge and a parsley sprig.

Nutritional Analysis per Serving

Calories 371 (Kilojoules 1,556); Total fat 15g; Saturated fat 2g; Protein 31g; Cholesterol 85mg; Carbohydrates 27g; Sodium 197mg; Dietary fibre 2g; Calories from fat 37%

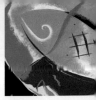

Blackened Catfish

2 teaspoons paprika

1 teaspoon cayenne pepper

1 teaspoon garlic powder

1 teaspoon dried thyme

½ teaspoon salt

1 teaspoon finely grated lemon rind

1 tablespoon olive oil

4 catfish fillets, about 125 g (4 oz) each

2 tablespoons lemon juice

Preparation: 10 minutes ✳ Cooking: 10 minutes ✳ Serves 4

The Cajun-style blackening technique is a terrific way to prepare these freshwater fish, and the same method can be used on other varieties of fish, skinless chicken breasts or pork chops. The spices blacken and season the fish as it cooks. Catfish is one of my favourite kinds of fish. Not only does it taste great, but it is an inexpensive source of protein.

✳ In a large shallow dish, combine the paprika, cayenne, garlic powder, thyme, salt and lemon rind. Add the catfish fillets and turn to coat both sides, pressing the herb-and-spice rub into the fish.

✳ In a large non-stick frying pan over a medium-high heat, heat the oil.

✳ Add the fish and cook for 4 minutes. Pour the lemon juice over the fillets, turn and cook until the fish just separates when pressed with a fork, about 4 minutes more.

✳ To serve, divide amongst 4 individual plates.

Nutritional Analysis per Serving

Calories 154 (Kilojoules 643); Total fat 7g; Saturated fat 1g; Protein 22g; Cholesterol 58mg; Carbohydrates 1g; Sodium 365mg; Dietary fibre 0g; Calories from fat 38%

2 teaspoons dark sesame oil

3 garlic cloves, very finely chopped

500 g (1 lb) skinless, boneless chicken
  breasts, cut into thin strips

1 tablespoon sesame seeds

60 g (2 oz) no-need-to-soak dried
  apricots, sliced

125 ml (4 fl oz) water

155 g (5 oz) apricot preserves

1 tablespoon reduced sodium soy sauce

1 tablespoon Dijon mustard

½ teaspoon grated fresh root ginger

250 g (8 oz) mangetouts, ends
  trimmed

Sesame Chicken and Mangetouts in Apricot Sauce

Preparation: 25 minutes ✳ Cooking: 20 minutes ✳ Serves 4

Apricots are an excellent source of beta-carotene, one of the anti-oxidants I encourage you to consume regularly for overall good health. Keep dried apricots on hand for snacks, especially in winter when the fresh ones are out of season. This sauce is so delicious that you'll want to try it without the chicken spooned over steamed vegetables or rice.

✳ In a large non-stick frying pan over a medium heat, heat the oil. Add the garlic and sauté for 1 minute. Add chicken and sauté until browned and no longer pink in the centre, about 5 minutes.

✳ Add the sesame seeds and sauté, stirring frequently, until browned, about 2 minutes. Add the apricots, water, apricot preserves, soy sauce, mustard and ginger and bring to the boil. Reduce the heat to low and simmer for 5 minutes. Add the mangetouts and simmer until tender-crisp, about 5 minutes more.

✳ To serve, divide amongst 4 individual plates.

Nutritional Analysis per Serving

Calories 270 (Kilojoules 1,140); Total fat 6g; Saturated fat 1g; Protein 34g;
Cholesterol 88mg; Carbohydrates 22g; Sodium 198mg; Dietary fibre 3g;
Calories from fat 19%

2 teaspoons olive oil

1 onion, chopped

3 garlic cloves, very finely chopped

1 green pepper, seeded, cored and
   sliced into thin strips

500 g (1 lb) boneless, skinless chicken
   breasts, cut into 2.5 cm (1 in) pieces

4 large tomatoes, peeled, seeded
   and chopped

1½ teaspoons curry powder

1 teaspoon ground cumin

1 teaspoon ground turmeric

¼ teaspoon ground ginger

¼ teaspoon salt

¼ teaspoon ground black pepper

75 g (2½ oz) virtually no fat plain
   yogurt

2 tablespoons chopped fresh coriander

Shopping Tip

∗ Fresh coriander adds a unique piquancy
to this Asian-spiced stew. If fresh
coriander is not available, use flat-leaf
parsley instead.

Curried Chicken Stew

Preparation: 30 minutes ∗ *Cooking: 25 minutes* ∗ *Serves 4*

The mild, intriguing curry sauce also works well with chunks of lean pork fillet, cooked the same way.

∗ In a large non-stick frying pan over a medium heat, heat the oil. Add the onion, garlic and pepper and sauté for 2 minutes. Add the chicken and sauté until browned and no longer pink in the centre, about 5 minutes. Add the tomatoes, curry, cumin, turmeric, ginger, salt and pepper. Bring to the boil, then reduce the heat to low and simmer for 15 minutes. Remove from the heat and add the yogurt and coriander. Stir to mix well.

∗ To serve, divide amongst 4 individual plates.

Nutritional Analysis per Serving

Calories 196 (Kilojoules 827); Total fat 4g; Saturated fat 1g; Protein 33g;
Cholesterol 88mg; Carbohydrates 8g; Sodium 236mg; Dietary fibre 2g;
Calories from fat 19%

1 turkey, about 5 kg (10 lb)

½ tablespoon salt

½ tablespoon ground black pepper

30 g (1 oz) margarine, melted

2 tablespoons chopped fresh rosemary

2 tablespoons chopped fresh thyme

2 tart apples, such as Granny Smith,
    cored and sliced

1 onion, sliced

Storage Tip

✳ To store fresh herbs, trim their stalks slightly; place in a jar or other container of fresh water, as you would cut flowers; and refrigerate. Trim the stalks and freshen the water daily. The herbs should keep for up to 1 week.

Roast Turkey

Preparation: 15 minutes ✳ *Cooking: 3 hours 20 minutes* ✳ *Serves 6*

To ensure proper cooking of a turkey, plan on about 20 minutes per 500 g (1 lb) for an unstuffed bird. I never cook stuffing or dressing inside poultry as it will absorb fat. If you're using an instant-read thermometer, do not insert it into the meat while it roasts; just use to test for doneness.

✳ Preheat the oven to 230°C (450°F/Gas 8). Coat the rack of a large roasting tin with non-stick cooking spray. Remove the giblets, heart, liver and neck from inside the turkey and reserve for another use.

✳ Rinse the bird inside and out, pat dry and sprinkle inside and out with the salt and pepper. Place the turkey, breast side up, on the rack in the tin.

✳ In a small bowl, combine the margarine, rosemary and thyme. Brush the turkey with the herb mixture. Insert a meat thermometer deep into the thickest part of the thigh, next to the body but not touching the bone. Spread the apple and onion slices round the bird.

✳ Place the turkey in the oven and immediately reduce the temperature to 180°C (350°F/Gas 4). Roast, basting every 15 minutes with the drippings, until the thermometer registers 75°C (175°F) and a drumstick moves easily in the joint, about 3 hours and 20 minutes.

✳ Transfer to a platter and discard the onion and apples. Cover the turkey with foil and let rest for 10–15 minutes. Remove the skin, carve and serve. One serving is 185 g (6 oz).

Nutritional Analysis per Serving

Calories 276 (Kilojoules 1,161); Total fat 8g; Saturated fat 2g; Protein 47g; Cholesterol 146mg; Carbohydrates 5g; Sodium 138mg; Dietary fibre 0g; Calories from fat 25%

500 g (1 lb) boneless, skinless chicken
   breasts, cut into 2.5 cm (1 in)
   pieces
1 red pepper, seeded, cored and
   chopped
1 yellow pepper, seeded, cored and
   chopped
1 onion, chopped
4 garlic cloves, very finely chopped
1 tablespoon cumin seeds
1 tablespoon chopped fresh oregano
1 teaspoon chilli powder
¼ teaspoon salt
¼ teaspoon ground black pepper
2 large tomatoes, peeled, seeded
   and chopped
440 g (14 oz) canned yellow hominy,
   (see introduction)
220 g (7 oz) cooked pinto beans
235 g (7½ oz) cooked rice
10 g (⅓ oz) fresh coriander, chopped
60 ml (2 fl oz) soured cream

Mexican Chicken Casserole

*Preparation: 25 minutes * Cooking: 1 hour * Serves 4*

*The combination of peppers, chilli powder and pinto beans inspired the
name of this easy-to-put-together dish, originally made from leftovers
Karen Averitt had around the kitchen in Montana. I loved the taste
and asked her to figure out what she had used so she could contribute it
to this book. The casserole can be assembled ahead, covered with cling
film and refrigerated for up to 2 days before baking. Usually sold in cans,
hominy is dried corn that has had the hull and germ removed. It is a
popular ingredient in Mexican and American Tex Mex cooking. Look for
it in health food shops. If you can only find the dried variety, however, it
has to be soaked and simmered like dried beans.*

✳ Preheat the oven to 180°C (350°F/Gas 4). Coat a 33 x 23 x 5 cm
(13 x 9 x 2 in) ovenproof dish with non-stick cooking spray.

✳ Coat a large non-stick frying pan with non-stick cooking
spray and place over a medium heat. Add the chicken, peppers,
onion, garlic, cumin seeds, oregano, chilli powder, salt and
pepper and sauté, stirring frequently, until the chicken is golden,
about 5 minutes. Add the tomatoes and simmer for 5 minutes.
Add the hominy, pinto beans and rice and cook for 5 minutes
more.

✳ Remove from the heat and add the coriander and soured
cream. Stir to mix well.

✳ Transfer to the prepared dish and bake until bubbly, about
45 minutes.

✳ To serve, divide amongst 4 individual plates.

Nutritional Analysis per Serving

Calories 454 (Kilojoules 1,917); Total fat 6g; Saturated fat 2g; Protein 41g;
Cholesterol 97mg; Carbohydrates 61g; Sodium 238mg; Dietary fibre 2g;
Calories from fat 12%

3 tablespoons chopped fresh sage

1 teaspoon paprika

1 teaspoon ground fennel seeds

¼ teaspoon cayenne pepper

¼ teaspoon ground black pepper

2 pheasants, about 1.5 kg (3 lb) each,
   rinsed and halved

1 tablespoon olive oil

1 small onion, chopped

3 garlic cloves, very finely chopped

250 ml (8 fl oz) Chicken Stock (recipe
   on page 206) or canned reduced
   sodium chicken broth

2 shallots, very finely chopped

60 ml (2 fl oz) balsamic vinegar

2 tablespoons soured cream

Roast Pheasant

*Preparation: 30 minutes * Cooking: 1 hour 20 minutes * Serves 4*

Game birds are lower in fat than chicken or turkey and contain none of the additives found in some brands of commercial poultry. We think the spices in this recipe really bring out the distinctive flavour of the pheasant. If pheasant isn't available, substitute game hens, capon or chicken.

✷ Preheat the oven to 180°C (350°F/Gas 4). Coat a shallow ovenproof dish with non-stick cooking spray.

✷ In a small bowl, combine the sage, paprika, fennel, cayenne and pepper. Rub the mixture evenly over the pheasants.

✷ In a large non-stick frying pan over a medium heat, heat the oil. Add the onion and half of the garlic and sauté, stirring frequently, until the onion is soft, about 2 minutes. Add the pheasants and sauté for 5 minutes. Turn and sauté until browned, about 5 minutes more.

✷ Transfer the pheasants to the prepared dish and top with half of the stock or broth. Roast, uncovered, basting with the pan juices every 15 minutes, until the juices run clear when the meat is pierced with a knife, 35–45 minutes.

✷ To make the sauce, coat the inside of a small saucepan with non-stick cooking spray and place over a medium heat. Add the shallots and the remaining garlic and sauté for 2 minutes. Add the balsamic vinegar and the remaining stock or broth, bring to the boil, reduce the heat to low and simmer until the sauce is reduced slightly and the shallots are soft, about 10 minutes.

✷ Transfer the pheasants to a serving platter and reserve the pan juices. Raise the heat under the sauce to medium. Add the pan juices and whisk until blended and simmering. Remove from the heat and whisk in the soured cream.

✷ To serve, remove the skin and top the meat with the sauce.

Nutritional Analysis per Serving

Calories 794 (Kilojoules 3,310); Total fat 46g; Saturated fat 15g; Protein 91g; Cholesterol 714mg; Carbohydrates 3g; Sodium 219mg; Dietary fibre 0g; Calories from fat 52%

250 ml (8 fl oz) Chicken Stock (recipe on page 206) or canned reduced sodium chicken broth

30 g (1 oz) dried cloud ear mushrooms or dried shiitake mushrooms, stalks removed

60 ml (2 fl oz) rice wine vinegar

2 tablespoons reduced sodium soy sauce

2 tablespoons honey

¼ teaspoon hot pepper flakes

2 teaspoons dark sesame oil

4 garlic cloves, very finely chopped

1 tablespoon finely chopped fresh root ginger

4 boneless pork loin chops, about 125 g (4 oz) each, trimmed of visible fat

Nutrition Tip

* Purchase cuts with *loin* or *leg* in the name; these are the leanest. Today's selection of pork products fits perfectly into a healthy lifestyle. These lean cuts trimmed of visible fat are lower in fat and lower in calories compared with the pork of just a decade ago.

Garlic Pork Chops with Black Mushrooms

*Preparation: 25 minutes * Cooking: 30 minutes * Serves 4*

Cloud ear mushrooms are usually sold dried and can be found in most supermarkets and speciality food shops or in Asian markets. If you find neither those nor shiitake mushrooms, substitute fresh button mushrooms. The sauce will not be as richly flavoured, but the overall dish will still be delicious.

* In a small saucepan over a medium heat, bring the stock or broth to the boil. Add the mushrooms, reduce the heat to low and simmer, uncovered, for 10 minutes.

* In a small bowl, combine the vinegar, soy sauce, honey and pepper flakes.

* In a large non-stick frying pan over a medium heat, heat the sesame oil. Add the garlic and ginger and sauté, stirring frequently, for 2 minutes. Add the chops and cook for 2 minutes. Turn and cook until browned, about 2 minutes more. Add the vinegar mixture and bring to the boil. Reduce the heat to low and simmer for 5 minutes.

* Using a slotted spoon, remove the mushrooms from the stock or broth and slice into thin strips. Reserve the liquid.

* Stir the mushrooms and reserved liquid into the pan with the chops, reduce the heat to low and simmer until the sauce is reduced and the chops are no longer pink in the centre, about 5 minutes.

* To serve, divide the chops amongst 4 individual plates. Top each with an equal amount of the mushroom sauce.

Nutritional Analysis per Serving

Calories 217 (Kilojoules 914); Total fat 7g; Saturated fat 1g; Protein 30g; Cholesterol 65mg; Carbohydrates 8g; Sodium 317mg; Dietary fibre 1g; Calories from fat 29%

Beef Fillet with Artichokes and Pearl Onions

Preparation: 25 minutes ✳ Cooking: 20 minutes ✳ Serves 4

When shopping for beef fillet, choose cuts with little visible fat and a bright red colour. Before cooking, trim any visible fat. A 125 g (4 oz) beef fillet will cook down to a 90 g (3 oz) serving, about the size of a deck of cards. Combine this main course with dishes that are very low in fat if you desire a meal with calories from fat of less than 25 per-cent.

1.5 litres (2½ pints) water

375 g (12 oz) pearl onions

1 tablespoon olive oil

5 artichoke hearts, quartered

1 red pepper, seeded, cored and
    thinly sliced

1 tablespoon chopped fresh thyme

½ tablespoon black peppercorns,
    cracked

4 pieces of beef fillet, about 125 g
    (4 oz) each, trimmed of visible fat

10 g (⅓ oz) fresh flat-leaf parsley,
    chopped

✳ In a medium saucepan over a high heat, bring the water to the boil. Add the onions and blanch for 5 minutes. Drain, rinse in cold water and remove the outer skin.

✳ In a large non-stick frying pan over a medium heat, heat the olive oil. Add the onions, artichokes, pepper and thyme and sauté, stirring frequently, until the onions and artichokes are golden and the pepper is tender-crisp, about 10 minutes. Using a slotted spoon, remove the vegetables from the pan and keep warm.

✳ Press the cracked pepper into both sides of the pieces of beef.

✳ Place the steaks in the hot pan and cook for 5 minutes. Turn and cook until the meat is dark brown on the outside and slightly pink in the centre for medium-rare, 3–5 minutes more.

✳ To serve, divide the beef amongst 4 individual plates. Top each with an equal amount of the vegetable mixture and parsley.

Nutrition Tip

✳ The recipe was designed using fresh or frozen artichoke hearts. If only marinated ones are available, drain and rinse them before using to reduce the fat from the oily marinade.

Nutritional Analysis per Serving

Calories 278 (Kilojoules 1,185); Total fat 11g; Saturated fat 4g; Protein 29g; Cholesterol 76mg; Carbohydrates 18g; Sodium 63mg; Dietary fibre 4g; Calories from fat 35%

75 g (2½ oz) unbleached plain flour

1 teaspoon dried oregano

1 teaspoon dried basil

1 teaspoon dried rosemary

1 teaspoon dried sage

1 teaspoon salt

1 teaspoon ground black pepper

2 kg (4½ lb) bison shanks or veal shanks, trimmed of visible fat and cut into 5 cm (2 in) pieces

1 tablespoon olive oil

10 g (⅓ oz) fresh rosemary, chopped

10 g (⅓ oz) fresh sage, chopped

2 tablespoons finely grated lemon rind

8 garlic cloves, very finely chopped

125 ml (4 fl oz) balsamic vinegar

750 ml (24 fl oz) Chicken Stock (recipe on page 206) or canned reduced sodium chicken broth

10 g (⅓ oz) fresh flat-leaf parsley, chopped

Nutrition Tip

✳ The marrow from the centre of the shank – a traditional delicacy enjoyed with osso buco – is very high in fat and should not be eaten as part of this recipe.

Bison Osso Buco

Preparation: 20 minutes ✱ *Cooking: 3 hours 10 minutes* ✱ *Serves 4*

This is actually our favourite special-occasion meal. Slow cooking over low heat makes this relatively inexpensive cut of meat quite tender. Substitute beef chuck or rump roast or veal, if desired, bearing in mind that their fat contents may be different than that shown for the bison.

✱ In a shallow glass dish, combine the flour, dried oregano, basil, rosemary, sage, salt and pepper. Add the bison or veal shanks and turn to coat well.

✱ In a large flameproof casserole over a medium heat, heat the oil. Add the bison or veal and sauté, stirring frequently, until browned, about 5 minutes. Add the fresh rosemary and sage, lemon rind and garlic and sauté, stirring frequently, for 2 minutes more. Add the vinegar and 250 ml (8 fl oz) of the stock or broth and simmer, uncovered, until the liquid is almost evaporated, about 20 minutes. Add the remaining stock or broth, cover, reduce the heat to low and simmer for 40 minutes more.

✱ Preheat the oven to 180°C (350°F/Gas 4).

✱ Cover the bison or veal and bake for 2 hours, spooning the sauce over the meat every 15 minutes.

✱ To serve, divide amongst 4 individual plates. Top each with an equal amount of the parsley.

Nutritional Analysis per Serving (for veal)

Calories 382 (Kilojoules 1,607); Total fat 10g; Saturated fat 3g; Protein 55g; Cholesterol 210mg; Carbohydrates 17g; Sodium 771mg; Dietary fibre 1g; Calories from fat 24%

4 garlic cloves, very finely chopped

2 shallots, very finely chopped

10 g (⅓ oz) fresh flat-leaf parsley, chopped

10 g (⅓ oz) fresh rosemary, chopped

125 ml (4 fl oz) unsalted beef stock

2 tablespoons reduced sodium soy sauce

60 ml (2 fl oz) lemon juice

1 tablespoon finely grated lemon rind

½ tablespoon black peppercorns

500 g (1 lb) bison fillet or beef sirloin, trimmed of visible fat

Nutrition Tip

✳ Shallots, even given the relatively small quantities in which they are included, provide good quantities of vitamin A.

Grilled Bison with Rosemary Marinade

Preparation: 15 minutes ✳ Cooking: 20 minutes ✳ Serves 4

In addition to the preparation time, you'll need to marinate the bison for at least 4 hours. Because there is not much fatty tissue in bison meat, it's important to marinate the fillet before cooking. The marinade tenderizes the meat fibres while adding a distinct, delicious flavour.

✳ To make the marinade, in a food processor with the metal blade or in a blender, combine the garlic, shallots, parsley, rosemary, broth, soy sauce, lemon juice, lemon rind and peppercorns and process until smooth.

✳ Place the bison or beef in a shallow non-metallic dish and pour in the marinade. Cover and refrigerate for 4 hours to 2 days, turning the meat occasionally.

✳ Prepare a fire in an outdoor barbecue or preheat the grill. Place the bison or beef on the barbecue or grill and discard the marinade. Grill the bison for 10 minutes or beef for 15 minutes. Turn and grill until the meat is medium-rare, 5–10 minutes more.

✳ To serve, slice and divide amongst 4 individual plates.

Nutritional Analysis per Serving (for beef)

Calories 183 (Kilojoules 769); Total fat 7g; Saturated fat 2g; Protein 28g; Cholesterol 0mg; Carbohydrates 3g; Sodium 184mg; Dietary fibre 0g; Calories from fat 33%

Spaghetti in Spicy Peanut Sauce

125 ml (4 fl oz) Vegetable Stock
   (recipe on page 207)

3 tablespoons reduced fat chunky
   peanut butter

1 tablespoon reduced sodium soy sauce

1 garlic clove, very finely chopped

¼ teaspoon crushed red pepper flakes

6 litres (10½ pints) water

375 g (12 oz) dried spaghetti

1 green pepper, seeded, cored and
   chopped

1 red pepper, seeded, cored and
   chopped

75 g (2½ oz) spring onions, green and
   white parts, chopped

10 g (⅓ oz) fresh coriander, chopped

Cooking Tip

✱ To test that pasta is done al dente, use
a long fork to remove a piece about
1 minute before the allotted cooking time.
Let it cool briefly, then taste. When al
dente it should be tender and cooked
through but still chewy.

*Preparation: 15 minutes * Cooking: 10 minutes * Serves 4*

Although peanut butter is high in fat, a little goes a long way in providing protein, fibre, B vitamins, minerals and an interesting taste to this vegetarian dish. For the best flavour and texture, purchase pasta made from semolina (durum wheat flour). Other pasta may be substituted for the classic round strands of spaghetti. If you choose to use fresh rather than dried pasta, cook it for about 3 minutes.

✱ In a small saucepan over a medium-high heat, heat the stock until hot, about 2 minutes.

✱ To make the sauce, in a medium bowl, combine the hot stock, peanut butter, soy sauce, garlic and red pepper flakes.

✱ In a large pan over a high heat, bring the water to the boil. Add the spaghetti and cook according to the packet instructions or until al dente, about 8 minutes. During the last minute of cooking, add the peppers and blanch for 1 minute. Drain.

✱ In a large bowl, combine the pasta and peppers and the sauce and toss to coat well.

✱ To serve, divide amongst 4 individual plates. Top each with an equal amount of the spring onions and coriander.

Nutritional Analysis per Serving

Calories 418 (Kilojoules 1,771); Total fat 8g; Saturated fat 1g; Protein 15g; Cholesterol 0mg; Carbohydrates 75g; Sodium 207mg; Dietary fibre 5g; Calories from fat 17%

2 teaspoons olive oil

1 small onion, chopped

2 garlic cloves, very finely chopped

2 tablespoons lemon juice

2 teaspoons finely grated lemon rind

220 g (7 oz) uncooked Arborio rice

750 ml (24 fl oz) Vegetable Stock
    (recipe on page 207)

125 g (4 oz) broccoli florets

155 g (5 oz) green peas

45 g (1½ oz) grated pecorino cheese

10 g (⅓ oz) fresh flat-leaf parsley,
    chopped

¼ teaspoon ground black pepper

Storage Tip

✻ The risotto can be stored, covered, in
the refrigerator for up to 2 days. Reheat
in a saucepan over a low heat, adding
more stock or water as necessary to
prevent sticking.

Lemon-Broccoli Risotto

Preparation: 20 minutes ✻ *Cooking: 35 minutes* ✻ *Serves 4*

*Arborio rice, a short-grained Italian variety found in well-stocked
supermarkets and delicatessens, gives risotto its unique, creamy texture.*

✻ In a large non-stick frying pan over a medium heat, heat the
oil. Add the onion and garlic and sauté until the onion is tender,
about 2 minutes. Add the lemon juice, lemon rind and rice and
sauté, stirring frequently, until the rice is golden, about 2 minutes.

✻ Add 125 ml (4 fl oz) of the stock, reduce the heat to low and
simmer until the liquid is absorbed, about 5 minutes. Continue
adding the stock, 125 ml (4 fl oz) at a time, stirring constantly
and waiting until each addition is absorbed before adding the
next, about 5 minutes. With the last 125 ml (4 fl oz) of stock, add
the broccoli and peas. Cook until the liquid is absorbed and the
broccoli and peas are tender, about 5 minutes.

✻ Remove from the heat, add the cheese, parsley and pepper and
stir until the cheese melts.

✻ To serve, divide amongst 4 individual plates.

Nutritional Analysis per Serving

Calories 310 (Kilojoules 1,298); Total fat 7g; Saturated fat 3g; Protein 13g;
Cholesterol 11mg; Carbohydrates 47g; Sodium 130mg; Dietary fibre 3g;
Calories from fat 21%

Linguine with Goat's Cheese, Tomatoes and Onions

2 teaspoons olive oil

2 onions, thinly sliced

1 tablespoon sugar

2 garlic cloves, very finely chopped

6 large tomatoes, peeled, seeded and chopped

10 g (⅓ oz) fresh basil, chopped

2 tablespoons chopped fresh oregano

¼ teaspoon ground black pepper

6 litres (10½ pints) water

375 g (12 oz) dried linguine

75 g (2½ oz) crumbled goat's cheese

Shopping Tip

∗ When tomatoes are out of season, substitute about 185 g (6 oz) of canned diced tomatoes for each large fresh tomato. Drain off the excess juice from the can before use.

Preparation: 25 minutes ∗ *Cooking: 25 minutes* ∗ *Serves 4*

The tomatoes give this dish a healthy dose of the anti-oxidant vitamin C and, along with the pasta, lots of fibre. Cheese made from goat's milk is chalky white and available in a variety of shapes and sizes. Young and fresh versions are mild and creamy; aged cheeses are stronger and drier. Either can be used to add a tangy taste to this vegetarian pasta dish.

∗ To make the sauce, in a large non-stick frying pan over a medium heat, heat the oil. Add the onions and sugar and sauté, stirring frequently, until the onions are golden, about 5 minutes. Add the garlic and sauté, stirring frequently, for 2 minutes more. Add the tomatoes, basil, oregano and pepper. Bring to the boil, reduce the heat to low and simmer until reduced slightly, about 5 minutes.

∗ In a large pot over high heat, bring the water to the boil. Add the linguine and cook according to the package directions or until al dente, 8–10 minutes. Drain.

∗ To serve, divide the linguine amongst 4 individual plates. Top each with an equal amount of the sauce and goat's cheese.

Nutritional Analysis per Serving

Calories 439 (Kilojoules 1,863); Total fat 8g; Saturated fat 3g; Protein 16g; Cholesterol 13mg; Carbohydrates 81g; Sodium 288mg; Dietary fibre 5g; Calories from fat 16%

1 onion, chopped

4 large tomatoes, peeled, seeded
  and chopped

10 g (⅓ oz) fresh basil, chopped

2 tablespoons chopped fresh thyme

2 tablespoons chopped fresh oregano

4 garlic cloves, peeled

315 g (10 oz) spinach, stalks trimmed

375 g (15 oz) ricotta cheese

250 g (8 oz) mozzarella cheese, grated

2 egg whites

½ teaspoon grated nutmeg

¼ teaspoon ground black pepper

6 litres (10½ pints) water

9 dried lasagna noodles

1 courgette, sliced

250 g (8 oz) fresh mushrooms, sliced

2 tablespoons freshly grated
  pecorino cheese

Storage Tip

✴ The casserole can be assembled ahead, covered with cling film or foil and refrigerated for up to 2 days or frozen in an airtight container for up to 1 month. Defrost in the refrigerator before baking.

Vegetable Lasagna

Preparation: 1 hour ✴ Cooking: 1 hour ✴ Serves 6

No one will miss the meat in this delectable vegetarian version of the classic Italian casserole. Although it is designed as a main dish, you can serve it as a side dish for 12. It's an especially good choice for a buffet supper or to make ahead and have on hand for a last-minute meal.

✴ Preheat the oven to 180°C (350°F/Gas 4). Coat a 33 x 23 cm (13 x 9 in) ovenproof dish with non-stick cooking spray.

✴ In a medium saucepan over a medium heat, combine the onion, tomatoes, basil, thyme and oregano. Bring to the boil, then reduce the heat to low and simmer, uncovered, until the sauce has thickened, about 10 minutes. Remove from the heat.

✴ In a food processor with the metal blade or in a blender, combine the garlic, spinach, ricotta, half of the mozzarella, the egg whites, nutmeg and pepper. Process until blended.

✴ In a large pan over a high heat, bring the water to the boil. Add the noodles and cook according to the packet instructions or until al dente, about 10 minutes. Drain.

✴ In the prepared dish, layer 3 noodles, half of the spinach mixture, half of the courgettes and mushroom slices and one-third of the tomato sauce. Repeat the layers, using 3 noodles, the remaining spinach mixture, the remaining courgette and mushroom slices and half of the remaining tomato sauce. Top with the remaining noodles, the remaining tomato sauce and the remaining mozzarella. Sprinkle with the pecorino cheese.

✴ Bake, uncovered, until bubbly and golden on top, about 45 minutes. Cool for 10 minutes before slicing.

✴ To serve, divide amongst 6 individual plates.

Nutritional Analysis per Serving

Calories 421 (Kilojoules 1,770); Total fat 18g; Saturated fat 11g; Protein 27g; Cholesterol 61mg; Carbohydrates 40g; Sodium 451mg; Dietary fibre 4g; Calories from fat 39%

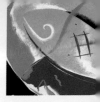

Bison Lasagna

Preparation: 45 minutes ✳ Cooking: 1¼ hours ✳ Serves 6

250 g (8 oz) minced bison or minced turkey

1 onion, chopped

8 garlic cloves, very finely chopped

2 large tomatoes, peeled, seeded and chopped

60 ml (2 fl oz) unsalted beef stock

2 tablespoons chopped fresh oregano

2 tablespoons chopped fresh rosemary

¼ teaspoon ground black pepper

500 g (1 lb) ricotta cheese

45 g (1½ oz) fresh basil, chopped

125 g (4 oz) sun-dried tomatoes, packed without oil, chopped

2 tablespoons grated Parmesan cheese

6 litres (10½ pints) water

9 dried lasagna noodles

185g (6 oz) mozzarella cheese, grated

✳ Preheat the oven to 180°C (350°F/Gas 4). Coat a 33 x 23 cm (13 x 9 in) dish with non-stick cooking spray.

✳ Coat a large non-stick frying pan with non-stick cooking spray and set over a medium heat. Add the bison or turkey, the onion and half of the garlic and sauté until the meat is browned and no longer pink, about 5 minutes. Stir in the chopped tomatoes, stock, oregano, rosemary and pepper. Bring to the boil, reduce the heat to low and simmer, uncovered, until the sauce has thickened, about 10 minutes. Remove from the heat.

✳ In a food processor with the metal blade or in a blender, combine the ricotta cheese, basil, sun-dried tomatoes, Parmesan cheese and remaining garlic. Process until smooth.

✳ In large pan over a high heat, bring the water to the boil. Add the noodles and cook according to the packet instructions or until al dente, about 10 minutes. Drain.

✳ In the prepared pan, layer 3 noodles, half of the ricotta mixture, one-third of the meat sauce and one-third of the mozzarella. Repeat the layers, using 3 noodles, the remaining ricotta mixture, half of the remaining meat sauce and half of the remaining mozzarella. Top with the remaining noodles, the remaining meat sauce and the remaining mozzarella.

✳ Bake, uncovered, until bubbly and golden on top, 35–45 minutes. Cool for 10 minutes before slicing.

✳ To serve, divide amongst 6 individual plates.

Nutritional Analysis per Serving (for turkey)

Calories 437 (Kilojoules 1,837); Total fat 18g; Saturated fat 10g; Protein 33g; Cholesterol 88mg; Carbohydrates 38g; Sodium 328mg; Dietary fibre 2g; Calories from fat 37%

2 teaspoons olive oil

8 garlic cloves, very finely chopped

2 small shallots, very finely chopped

4 large tomatoes, peeled, seeded and
diced

1 tablespoon chopped fresh oregano

½ teaspoon crushed red pepper flakes

½ teaspoon salt

6 litres (10½ pints) water

375 g (12 oz) dried penne pasta

10 g (⅓ oz) fresh flat-leaf parsley,
chopped

2 tablespoons grated pecorino cheese

Cooking Tip

✽ For a dish in the style of pasta
primavera, stir steamed fresh vegetables,
such as broccoli, asparagus, green peas
and peppers, into the tomato sauce
before spooning over the pasta.

Penne with Garlic-Tomato Sauce

Preparation: 15 minutes ✽ Cooking: 30 minutes ✽ Serves 4

*I always ask that this sauce recipe be doubled or tripled and put into jars
in the refrigerator so that I can use it to top pasta, rice, polenta or even
potatoes as a very quick late-night supper.*

✽ In a large non-stick frying pan over a medium heat, heat the oil.
Add the garlic and shallots and sauté until tender, about 3 minutes.

✽ Add the tomatoes and oregano, bring to the boil, then reduce
the heat to low and simmer for 10 minutes. Add the red pepper
flakes and salt and simmer for 5 minutes more. Keep warm.

✽ In a large pan over a high heat, bring the water to the boil.
Add the penne and cook according to the packet instructions or
until al dente, 8–10 minutes. Drain. Add the penne to the frying
pan and stir to coat well.

✽ To serve, divide amongst 4 individual plates. Top each with an
equal amount of the parsley and cheese.

Nutritional Analysis per Serving

**Calories 385 (Kilojoules 1,634); Total fat 5g; Saturated fat 1g; Protein 14g;
Cholesterol 4mg; Carbohydrates 75g; Sodium 300mg; Dietary fibre 4g;
Calories from fat 12%**

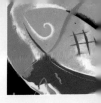

1 tablespoon grated Parmesan cheese

375 g (12 oz) spinach, stalks trimmed

2 shallots, halved

45 g (1½ oz) margarine

45 g (1½ oz) unbleached plain flour

375 ml (12 fl oz) skimmed milk

6 egg whites

¼ teaspoon cream of tartare

125 g (4 oz) Emmenthal cheese, grated

1 teaspoon chilli powder

¼ teaspoon grated nutmeg

Cooking Tip

✳ Although shallots resemble garlic cloves in size and shape, they may be easily peeled for slicing and chopping like an onion. Simply trim off their stalk and root ends, then slit their thin papery skins to remove them.

Spinach Soufflé

Preparation: 30 minutes ✳ Cooking: 35 minutes ✳ Serves 4

This soufflé, rich in iron and beta-carotene, is my absolute favourite; it pairs very nicely with the hearty Ratatouille (recipe on page 198). Serve soufflés immediately after removing from the oven as the puff collapses upon cooling.

✳ Preheat the oven to 190°C (375°F/Gas 5). Coat a 2 litre (3½ pint) soufflé dish with non-stick cooking spray.

✳ Sprinkle the Parmesan cheese into the dish and turn to coat the base and sides. Place the dish on a large baking sheet.

✳ In a steaming basket in a saucepan filled with 2.5 cm (1 in) of water over a medium heat, steam the spinach until tender, about 3 minutes. Remove from the basket; squeeze to remove all liquid.

✳ In a food processor with the metal blade or in a blender, combine the spinach and shallots and process until finely chopped.

✳ In a large non-stick frying pan over a low heat, melt the margarine. Add the flour and stir constantly with a wire whisk until blended, about 2 minutes. Increase the heat to medium and gradually add the milk, stirring constantly with a wire whisk, and cook until the mixture boils, about 5 minutes.

✳ Reduce the heat to low, add the spinach mixture and cook until the mixture begins to simmer, about 3 minutes.

✳ In a large bowl, using an electric mixer on high speed, beat the egg whites until foamy. Add the cream of tartar and beat on high speed until stiff peaks form.

✳ In a large bowl, combine one-fourth of the egg whites, the cheese, chilli powder, nutmeg and the spinach mixture and whisk to mix well. Fold in the remaining egg whites. Pour into the prepared dish and bake until puffed and set, 30–35 minutes.

✳ To serve, divide amongst 4 individual plates.

Nutritional Analysis per Serving

Calories 327 (Kilojoules 1,363); Total fat 20g; Saturated fat 8g; Protein 21g; Cholesterol 32mg; Carbohydrates 16g; Sodium 518mg; Dietary fibre 3g; Calories from fat 55%

220 g (7 oz) dried black beans

1 litre (1¾ pints) water

2 teaspoons olive oil

1 large onion, chopped

3 garlic cloves, very finely chopped

1½ teaspoons chilli powder

1 teaspoon ground cumin

2 large tomatoes, peeled, seeded and chopped

185 g (6 oz) sweetcorn kernels

3 jalapeño chillies, seeded and chopped

¼ teaspoon salt

¼ teaspoon ground black pepper

8 corn tortillas, 15 cm (6 in) in diameter

125 ml (4 fl oz) soured cream

60 g (2 oz) reduced fat Cheddar cheese, grated

Tomato Salsa

2 tomatoes, seeded and chopped

30 g (1 oz) red onion, chopped

1 jalapeño chilli, seeded and diced

1 tablespoon chopped fresh coriander

1 teaspoon lime juice

⅛ teaspoon salt

⅛ teaspoon ground black pepper

Black Bean Enchiladas with Tomato Salsa

*Preparation: 20 minutes * Cooking: 2 hours * Serves 4*

Pair this vegetarian main dish with rice, as combined portions of beans and rice provide the complete protein but none of the fat of a meat-based meal.

✳ In a large saucepan over a high heat, combine the beans and water and bring to the boil. Reduce the heat to medium and cook for 1½ hours, skimming away the grey foam. Drain well.

✳ Preheat the oven to 180°C (350°F/Gas 4). Coat a 33 x 23 cm (13 x 9 in) ovenproof dish with non-stick cooking spray.

✳ In a large non-stick frying pan over a medium heat, heat the oil. Add the onion and garlic and sauté for 3 minutes. Add the chilli powder and cumin and sauté for 1 minute. Add half of the tomatoes and the sweetcorn, chillies, salt and pepper and simmer for 1 minute.

✳ Wrap the tortillas in aluminium foil and warm in the oven for 5 minutes.

✳ In a food processor with the metal blade, combine the beans and soured cream and process until smooth. Add to the frying pan and cook until the beans are warm, about 3 minutes.

✳ Divide the bean mixture amongst the tortillas. Roll and place seam side down in the prepared dish. Top with the remaining tomatoes and the cheese. Cover with aluminium foil and bake until the cheese melts, about 20 minutes.

✳ To serve, divide amongst 4 individual plates. Top each with an equal amount of the Tomato Salsa.

Tomato Salsa

✳ In a medium bowl, combine the tomatoes, onion, chilli, coriander, lime juice, salt and pepper. Stir to mix well. Cover and refrigerate until serving. One serving is 90 g (3 oz).

Nutritional Analysis per Serving

Calories 547 (Kilojoules 2,312); Total fat 14g; Saturated fat 7g; Protein 28g; Cholesterol 28mg; Carbohydrates 82g; Sodium 649mg; Dietary fibre 8g; Calories from fat 23%

Completing the Meal

250 g (8 oz) strawberries,
    hulled
2 bananas, peeled
375 ml (12 fl oz) cranberry juice
250 g (8 oz) crushed ice

Strawberry-Banana Shake

*Preparation: 10 minutes * Serves 4*

Shakes and smoothies are my morning drink of choice. This sweet-tart version is packed with fresh-fruit goodness. If you haven't already, add cranberry juice to your juice repertoire. It is an ample source of vitamin C and aids in flushing toxins from the body.

✳ In a food processor with the metal blade or in a blender, combine the strawberries, bananas and cranberry juice and process until smooth. Add the crushed ice and process until smooth.

✳ To serve, divide amongst 4 individual glasses.

Nutritional Analysis per Serving

Calories 108 (Kilojoules 456); Total fat 0.5g; Saturated fat 0g; Protein 1g; Cholesterol 0mg; Carbohydrates 26g; Sodium 11mg; Dietary fibre 1g; Calories from fat 3%

250 g (8 oz) orange sherbet or
    frozen yogurt
125 g (4 oz) strawberries,
    hulled
250 g (8 oz) pineapple chunks
375 ml (12 fl oz) sparkling
    mineral water

Sunshine Smoothie

*Preparation: 10 minutes * Serves 4*

As the name implies, this smoothie gets your day off to a sunny start, fulfilling 2 fruit servings of your recommended daily food requirements before you've left the house. If you're in a hurry and must eat on the run, take this healthy breakfast drink in an insulated cup to drink while you drive.

✳ In a food processor with the metal blade or in a blender, combine the sherbet or yogurt, strawberries and pineapple and process until smooth. Add the water and process until blended.

✳ To serve, divide amongst 4 individual glasses.

Nutritional Analysis per Serving

Calories 60 (Kilojoules 256); Total fat 0.5g; Saturated fat 0g; Protein 3g; Cholesterol 1mg; Carbohydrates 12g; Sodium 49mg; Dietary fibre 1g; Calories from fat 4%

960 ml (32 fl oz) skimmed milk

3 tablespoons sugar

4 teaspoons cocoa

1 teaspoon vanilla essence

Iced Cocoa

❋ For a low fat chocolate dessert, freeze the Hot Cocoa. When the mixture is firm, process in a food processor with the metal blade or in a blender until smooth. To serve, spoon into dessert bowls.

960 ml (32 fl oz) strong, freshly brewed coffee

250 ml (8 fl oz) skimmed milk

4 tablespoons icing sugar

2 tablespoons cocoa

1 teaspoon vanilla essence

Iced Skinny Café Mocha

❋ For a refreshingly cool drink, pour the Skinny Café Mocha into a heatproof glass container and cool. Cover and refrigerate for 4 hours. To serve, spoon shaved ice into tall glasses. Top with the chilled coffee.

Hot Cocoa

Preparation: 5 minutes ❋ *Serves 4*

It is hard to believe – but true – that one serving of this cocoa contains just 2 g of fat. Serve it piping hot as a breakfast beverage or iced as a dessert (recipe at left).

❋ In a small saucepan over a medium heat, warm the milk until bubbles just begin to appear around the edge, about 5 minutes. Gradually add the sugar, cocoa and vanilla and whisk until dissolved and blended.

❋ To serve, divide amongst 4 individual mugs.

Nutritional Analysis per Serving

Calories 142 (Kilojoules 603); Total fat 2g; Saturated fat 1g; Protein 9g; Cholesterol 5mg; Carbohydrates 25g; Sodium 190mg; Dietary fibre 0g; Calories from fat 10%

Skinny Café Mocha

Preparation: 15 minutes ❋ *Serves 4*

Fancy coffee bars serve low fat versions of their mocha-flavoured coffees and now you can, too. On a hot afternoon, the iced version (recipe at left) will clear your head and give you an energy boost.

❋ In a medium saucepan over a low heat, combine the coffee, milk, sugar and cocoa. Simmer until the sugar is dissolved, about 5 minutes. Remove from the heat and stir in the vanilla.

❋ To serve, divide amongst 4 individual mugs.

Nutritional Analysis per Serving

Calories 58 (Kilojoules 247); Total fat 1g; Saturated fat 0.5g; Protein 3g; Cholesterol 1mg; Carbohydrates 10.5g; Sodium 66mg; Dietary fibre 0g; Calories from fat 11%

960 ml (32 fl oz) tomato juice

2 tablespoons lemon juice

1½ teaspoons Worcestershire sauce

½ teaspoon ground celery seed

1 teaspoon drained, grated horseradish

¼ teaspoon ground black pepper

4 celery stalks

1 tablespoon chopped fresh flat-leaf
parsley

Tangy Tomato Drink

*Preparation: 15 minutes * Serves 4*

Mixing your own tomato juice cocktail allows you to control what's in it. Many similar commercial drinks are loaded with salt, MSG and other additives. The health benefits derived from this version outweigh the few moments it takes to put together.

✳ In a large pitcher, combine the tomato juice, lemon juice, Worcestershire sauce, celery seed, horseradish and pepper. Stir to mix well.

✳ To serve, divide amongst 4 individual glasses. Garnish each with a celery stalk and an equal amount of the parsley.

Nutritional Analysis per Serving

Calories 39 (Kilojoules 171); Total fat 0g; Saturated fat 0g; Protein 2g; Cholesterol 0mg; Carbohydrates 8g; Sodium 594mg; Dietary fibre 2g; Calories from fat 4%

960 ml (32 fl oz) non-alcohol apple
cider

1 tart apple, peeled, cored and sliced

2 lemon slices

1 vanilla pod, 2.5cm (1in) long

5 whole cloves

4 whole cinnamon sticks

Hot Fruit Cider

*Preparation: 10 minutes * Cooking: 10 minutes * Serves 4*

Cider is available with and without alcohol. If possible, use cider made from organic apples. The taste is sensational. You can substitute apple juice, although the flavour will be somewhat less fruity.

✳ In a medium saucepan over a medium heat, combine the cider, apple slices, lemon slices, vanilla pod and cloves. Bring to the boil, then reduce the heat to low, cover and simmer for 10 minutes. Remove from the heat and strain to remove the solids.

✳ To serve, divide amongst 4 individual mugs. Garnish each with a cinnamon stick.

Nutritional Analysis per Serving

Calories 50 (Kilojoules 215); Total fat 0g; Saturated fat 0g; Protein 0g; Cholesterol 0mg; Carbohydrates 11g; Sodium 8mg; Dietary fibre 0g; Calories from fat 0%

Salad Greens

An abundant range of greens exists to add wide variety to your salad bowls: lettuces, including tender butter lettuces (such as Boston, Bibb and limestone), crisp cos, and red leaf or oak leaf; curly endive, with its bitter edge; dark-green, peppery rocket; refreshingly bitter chicory; crisp, bitter, deep-purple radicchio; and familiar spinach, watercress and cabbages. Seek them out at a well-stocked supermarket or greengrocer. Separate, wash and dry thoroughly before refrigerating. The dressings shown at left are listed below and on page 184.

Dill Dressing

250 g (8 oz) virtually no fat plain yogurt

10 g (⅓ oz) fresh dill, chopped

2 teaspoons red wine vinegar

¼ teaspoon ground black pepper

Preparation: 10 minutes ✳ *Serves 8*

✳ In a small bowl, combine the yogurt, dill, vinegar and pepper and whisk until blended.

✳ Store in an airtight container in the refrigerator for up to 3 days. One serving is 2 tablespoons.

Nutritional Analysis per Serving

Calories 18 (Kilojoules 76); Total fat 0g; Saturated fat 0g; Protein 2g; Cholesterol 1mg; Carbohydrates 2g; Sodium 26mg; Dietary fibre 0g; Calories from fat 13%

Basil Dressing

125 ml (4 fl oz) buttermilk

125 g (4 oz) soured cream

10 g (⅓ oz) fresh basil, chopped

2 teaspoons white wine vinegar

⅛ teaspoon ground white pepper

⅛ teaspoon cayenne pepper

Preparation: 10 minutes ✳ *Serves 8*

✳ In a small bowl, combine the buttermilk, soured cream, basil, vinegar, pepper and cayenne and whisk until blended. Cover and refrigerate until ready to serve. Store in an airtight container in the refrigerator for up to 3 days. One serving is 2 tablespoons.

Nutritional Analysis per Serving

Calories 39 (Kilojoules 161); Total fat 3g; Saturated fat 2g; Protein 1g; Cholesterol 10mg; Carbohydrates 1.5g; Sodium 15mg; Dietary fibre 0g; Calories from fat 75%

125 ml (4 fl oz) rice vinegar

2 tablespoons reduced sodium
    soy sauce

2 tablespoons sesame seeds,
    lightly toasted

1 teaspoon dark sesame oil

1 garlic clove, very finely chopped

½ teaspoon grated fresh root ginger

Cooking Tip

To toast sesame seeds, spread on a baking sheet and bake in a preheated 180°C (350°F/Gas 4) oven, stirring occasionally, until golden, about 5 minutes.

1 teaspoon sugar

125 ml (4 fl oz) red wine vinegar

2 tablespoons Dijon mustard

2 tablespoons chopped fresh flat-leaf
    parsley

1 tablespoon olive oil

1 tablespoon water

¼ teaspoon ground black pepper

Nutrition Tip

✳ The greatest source of fat in many salads comes from the dressing. To get the most flavour but the least fat in your salad, serve the dressing on the side, dipping your fork into it before skewering the greens.

Sesame Garlic Dressing

Preparation: 10 minutes ✳ *Serves 8*

This Asian-influenced dressing is rich with the taste of sesame. Toasting the sesame seeds brings out their nutty flavour.

✳ In a small bowl, combine the vinegar, soy sauce, sesame seeds, sesame oil, garlic and ginger and whisk until blended.

✳ Cover and refrigerate until ready to serve. Store in an airtight container in the refrigerator for up to 3 days. One serving is 2 tablespoons.

Nutritional Analysis per Serving

Calories 27 (Kilojoules 113); Total fat 2g; Saturated fat 0g; Protein 1g; Cholesterol 0mg; Carbohydrates 1g; Sodium 2mg; Dietary fibre 0g; Calories from fat 68%

Mustard Vinaigrette

Preparation: 10 minutes ✳ *Serves 12*

Dijon mustard, whether made in Dijon, France, or made in the style of that region, is a pale yellow condiment made from a mixture of black or brown mustard seeds, white wine, vinegar, water and salt. It adds zest to this simple vinaigrette.

✳ In a small bowl, dissolve the sugar in the vinegar. Add the mustard, parsley, olive oil, water and pepper and whisk until blended.

✳ Cover and refrigerate until ready to serve. Store in an airtight container in the refrigerator for up to 2 weeks. One serving is 1 tablespoon.

Nutritional Analysis per Serving

Calories 16 (Kilojoules 65); Total fat 1g; Saturated fat 0g; Protein 0g; Cholesterol 0mg; Carbohydrates 1g; Sodium 75mg; Dietary fibre 0g; Calories from fat 63%

1 teaspoon honey

250 ml (8 fl oz) lukewarm water

2 teaspoons dried yeast

2 tablespoons olive oil

1 teaspoon salt

235 g (7½ oz) semolina flour

235 g (7½ oz) wholewheat flour

Storage Tip

✴ This dough can be made ahead and frozen for up to 2 months. After the first rising, wrap in cling film and aluminium foil and place in the freezer. Thaw at room temperature and follow the recipe from the second kneading.

Karen's Pizza Dough

Preparation: 25 minutes ✴ Makes 500 g (1lb)

In addition to the preparation time, allow 1½ hours for the dough to rise. This dough is easy to work with and tastes just great. Use it as a base for the pizzas beginning on page 107 or for your own creative versions.

✴ In a food processor with the metal blade or in a large bowl, combine the honey and water. Add the yeast to the water and let stand 5 minutes. Add the oil, salt and flours and process or stir until the mixture forms a ball, about 30 seconds by machine or 5 minutes by hand.

✴ Turn on to a lightly floured work surface and knead until the dough is smooth and elastic, about 5 minutes.

✴ Coat a large bowl with non-stick cooking spray, add the dough and turn to coat all sides. Cover with cling film and let rise in a warm place, free from draughr, until doubled in bulk, about 1 hour.

✴ Return to the lightly floured work surface and using your fist, punch down the dough, then knead for 2 minutes. Return to the bowl, cover with cling film and let rise again for 30 minutes.

✴ Use the dough according to recipe instructions. One serving is 125g (4oz).

Nutritional Analysis per Serving

Calories 445 (Kilojoules 1,886); Total fat 8g; Saturated fat 1g; Protein 15g; Cholesterol 0mg; Carbohydrates 84g; Sodium 501mg; Dietary fibre 6.5g; Calories from fat 16%

375 g (¾ lb) fresh spinach, stems
   removed and leaves chopped
250 g (8 oz) low fat cottage cheese
125 ml (4 fl oz) soured cream
1 tablespoon chopped fresh flat-leaf
   parsley
2 shallots, very finely chopped
¼ teaspoon salt
¼ teaspoon ground white pepper
250 g (8 oz) water chestnuts, drained
   and sliced

Creamy Spinach Spread

Preparation: 10 minutes ✳ Serves 12

Serve this dip on French bread or with fresh vegetables like cherry tomatoes, carrot and celery sticks, cucumber slices, courgette slices and broccoli and cauliflower florets.

✳ In a food processor with the metal blade or in a blender, combine the spinach, cottage cheese, soured cream, parsley, shallots, salt and pepper. Process until almost smooth. Transfer to a large bowl, add the water chestnuts and stir to mix well.

✳ Store in an airtight container in the refrigerator for up to 3 days. One serving is 2 tablespoons.

Nutritional Analysis per Serving

Calories 53 (Kilojoules 220); Total fat 2.5g; Saturated fat 1.5g; Protein 4g; Cholesterol 7mg; Carbohydrates 3.5g; Sodium 165mg; Dietary fibre 1g; Calories from fat 44%

250 g (8 oz) low fat soft cheese
250 g (8 oz) low fat cottage cheese
90 g (3 oz) mango chutney
10 g (⅓ oz) fresh flat-leaf parsley,
   chopped
2 tablespoons snipped fresh chives
2 teaspoons Dijon mustard
¼ teaspoon ground black pepper
⅛ teaspoon cayenne pepper

Chive Chutney Dip

Preparation: 10 minutes ✳ Serves 8

If you are having trouble finding healthy, tasty snacks, your search is over. Make this low fat herb-fruit dip and keep it in the refrigerator ready to enjoy with peeled and sliced carrots, celery, cucumbers and other vegetables.

✳ In a food processor with the metal blade or in a blender, combine the cheese, cottage cheese, chutney, parsley, chives, mustard, black pepper and cayenne. Process until smooth.

✳ Transfer the dip to a serving bowl, cover and refrigerate until ready to serve. Store in the refrigerator for up to one week. One serving is 60 g (2 oz).

Nutritional Analysis per Serving

Calories 86 (Kilojoules 363); Total fat 3g; Saturated fat 0g; Protein 9g; Cholesterol 2mg; Carbohydrates 8g; Sodium 299mg; Dietary fibre 0g; Calories from fat 26%

Caponata

Preparation: 20 minutes ✳ Cooking: 30 minutes ✳ Serves 12

Caponata is a traditional Italian starter, served as part of many antipasto arrays, and is made from a base of aubergine and tomatoes. Serve with the wholewheat bread, low fat crackers or toasted pitta wedges.

1 large aubergine (about 500g/
    1lb), unpeeled and cut into
    2.5 cm (1 in) cubes
2 teaspoons olive oil
1 onion, diced
2 garlic cloves, very finely chopped
2 celery stalks, chopped
2 tomatoes, chopped
60 ml (2 fl oz) red wine vinegar
6 large black olives, stoned and sliced
1½ tablespoons drained capers
2 tablespoons chopped fresh oregano
¼ teaspoon ground black pepper
2 tablespoons chopped fresh flat-leaf
    parsley
24 slices wholewheat bread

✳ Preheat the oven to 200°C (400°F/Gas 4). Coat a baking sheet with non-stick cooking spray.

✳ Spread the aubergine cubes on the baking sheet in a single layer. Bake for 15 minutes, turning halfway through the cooking time. Remove from the oven and set aside.

✳ In a large non-stick frying pan over a medium heat, heat the oil. Add the onion, garlic and celery and sauté until tender, about 5 minutes.

✳ Add the baked aubergine, tomatoes, vinegar, olives, capers, oregano and pepper. Bring to the boil, then reduce the heat to low and simmer until the caponata thickens, about 10 minutes. Remove from the heat and stir in the parsley.

✳ To serve, transfer to a serving bowl. Store in an airtight container in the refrigerator for up to 3 days. One serving is 2 slices of bread, each topped with 2 tablespoons of caponata.

Nutritional Analysis per Serving

Calories 171 (Kilojoules 724); Total fat 3g; Saturated fat 0.5g; Protein 7g; Cholesterol 0mg; Carbohydrates 31g; Sodium 435mg; Dietary fibre 5g; Calories from fat 15%

900 g (30 oz) cooked chick-peas
    beans, rinsed and drained

3 garlic cloves, very finely chopped

60 ml (2 fl oz) lemon juice

2 tablespoons tahini (sesame paste)

1 teaspoon ground cumin

1 teaspoon paprika

½ teaspoon finely grated lemon rind

½ teaspoon salt

4 pitta breads, quartered

Hummus with Pitta Bread

Preparation: 10 minutes ✳ *Serves 4*

✳ In a food processor with the metal blade or in a blender, combine the chick-peas, garlic, lemon juice, tahini, cumin, paprika, lemon rind and salt. Process until smooth.

✳ To serve, use as a spread or dip with the pitta bread. Makes 875 g (28 oz). One serving is 2 tablespoons hummus and 1 pitta bread. Store the hummus in an airtight container in the refrigerator for up to 3 days.

🗒 *Nutritional Analysis per Serving*

Calories 492 (Kilojoules 2,083); Total fat 7g; Saturated fat 1g; Protein 27g; Cholesterol 0mg; Carbohydrates 85g; Sodium 603mg; Dietary fibre 14g; Calories from fat 13%

2 teaspoons olive oil

2 small shallots, very finely chopped

1 garlic clove, minced

375 g (12 oz) fresh mushrooms, sliced

60 ml (2 fl oz) Chicken Stock
    (recipe on page 206) or canned
    reduced sodium chicken broth

2 tablespoons chopped fresh flat-leaf
    parsley

1 tablespoon chopped fresh thyme

¼ teaspoon salt

¼ teaspoon ground black pepper

250 g (8 oz) sourdough bread, cut
    into eight 2.5 cm (1 in) thick
    slices, toasted

Mushroom-Topped Crostini

Preparation: 15 minutes ✳ *Cooking: 15 minutes* ✳ *Serves 4*

✳ In a large non-stick frying pan over a medium heat, heat the oil. Add the shallots and garlic and sauté until tender, about 2 minutes. Add the mushrooms and sauté for 5 minutes.

✳ Add the stock or broth, parsley, thyme, salt and pepper and simmer until the liquid evaporates, about 5 minutes. Remove from the heat and cool.

✳ Transfer the mixture to a food processor with the metal blade or to a blender and process into fine pieces.

✳ To serve, spread 2 tablespoons of the mushroom topping on each bread slice. One serving is 2 slices. Store the topping in an airtight container in the refrigerator for up to 3 days.

🗒 *Nutritional Analysis per Serving*

Calories 185 (Kilojoules 783); Total fat 4g; Saturated fat 1g; Protein 7g; Cholesterol 0mg; Carbohydrates 33g; Sodium 476mg; Dietary fibre 2g; Calories from fat 18%

155 g (5 oz) yellow cornmeal

155 g (5 oz) unbleached plain flour

2 teaspoons baking powder

½ teaspoon bicarbonate of soda

¾ teaspoon salt

¼ teaspoon cayenne pepper

2 egg whites

250 ml (8 fl oz) buttermilk

2 tablespoons corn oil

2 tablespoons honey

185 g (6 oz) sweetcorn

45g (1½oz) reduced fat Cheddar
cheese

3 green chillies, seeded and chopped

1 tablespoon chopped pimientos
(sweet peppers)

Shopping Tip

✱ Both green chillies and pimientos are available already seeded and chopped in cans and bottles, greatly lessening the preparation time of this bread.

Chilli Cheese Corn Bread

Preparation: 20 minutes ✱ *Cooking: 25 minutes* ✱ *Serves 8*

This moist, flavourful bread makes a substantial side dish for soups and salads. The buttermilk used here replaces the soured cream in traditional Texan versions, greatly lowering the fat without lessening the taste.

✱ Preheat the oven to 200°C (400°F/Gas 6). Coat a 23 cm (9 in) round cake tin with non-stick cooking spray.

✱ In a large bowl, combine the cornmeal, flour, baking powder, bicarbonate of soda, salt and cayenne pepper. Make a well in the centre.

✱ In a medium bowl, combine the egg whites, buttermilk, oil and honey and whisk until blended. Add the corn, cheese, chillies and pimientos and stir to mix well. Pour the egg mixture into the well in the dry ingredients and stir until just combined.

✱ Pour the mixture into the prepared tin and bake until a cocktail stick inserted in the centre comes out clean, about 20 minutes. Cool in the pan before slicing.

✱ To serve, cut into 8 pieces. One serving is one piece. Store wrapped in cling film in the refrigerator for up to 3 days.

Nutritional Analysis per Serving

Calories 235 (Kilojoules 988); Total fat 5g; Saturated fat 1g; Protein 8g; Cholesterol 3mg; Carbohydrates 41g; Sodium 507mg; Dietary fibre 1g; Calories from fat 19%

250g (8oz) whole chestnuts, unshelled
1 tablespoon olive oil
1 shallot, very finely chopped
1 garlic clove, very finely chopped
375 g (12 oz) spinach, stalks trimmed
1 tablespoon balsamic vinegar
¼ teaspoon ground black pepper

Nutrition Tip

✳ Chestnuts are lower in fat than many counterparts in the nut family. Roasting brings out their flavour, while softening their texture. Toss chestnuts into your favourite salads, rice and pasta dishes for added protein and flavour.

500 g (1 lb) baby carrots
2 tablespoons chopped fresh dill
2 tablespoons orange juice
1 tablespoon olive oil
½ teaspoon finely grated lemon rind
¼ teaspoon mustard powder
¼ teaspoon salt
⅛ teaspoon ground black pepper

Spinach and Roasted Chestnuts

Preparation: 25 minutes ✳ *Cooking: 30 minutes* ✳ *Serves 4*

✳ Preheat the oven to 200°C (400°F/Gas 6).

✳ Using a sharp knife, cut an X in the flat side of each chestnut and spread the nuts in the base of a roasting tin. Roast until the shells split, 15–20 minutes. Cool to the touch. Remove and discard the shells and inner brown skin.

✳ In a large non-stick frying pan over a medium heat, heat the oil. Add the shallot and garlic and sauté, stirring frequently, for 2 minutes. Add the spinach and vinegar and sauté, stirring frequently, until the spinach wilts, about 5 minutes. Add the pepper and chestnuts and sauté until the chestnuts are warm, about 5 minutes.

✳ To serve, divide amongst 4 individual plates.

Nutritional Analysis per Serving

Calories 140 (Kilojoules 588); Total fat 5g; Saturated fat 1g; Protein 4g; Cholesterol 0mg; Carbohydrates 21g; Sodium 137mg; Dietary fibre 4g; Calories from fat 32%

Steamed Carrots with Dill

Preparation: 15 minutes ✳ *Cooking: 10 minutes* ✳ *Serves 4*

✳ Fill a medium saucepan with 2.5 cm (1in) of water, set a steamer basket inside and place over a medium heat. Add the carrots and steam until tender-crisp, 8–10 minutes.

✳ In a medium bowl, combine the dill, orange juice, olive oil, lemon rind, mustard, salt and pepper and whisk until blended.

✳ In a large bowl, combine the carrots and dill mixture and toss to mix well.

✳ To serve, divide amongst 4 individual plates.

Nutritional Analysis per Serving

Calories 67 (Kilojoules 276); Total fat 4g; Saturated fat 1g; Protein 1g; Cholesterol 0mg; Carbohydrates 8g; Sodium 179mg; Dietary fibre 3g; Calories from fat 47%

Grilled Summer Vegetables

2 tablespoons rice wine vinegar

1 tablespoon olive oil

1 tablespoon reduced sodium soy sauce

1 tablespoon Dijon mustard

1 tablespoon honey

1 red pepper, seeded, cored and quartered

1 green pepper, seeded, cored and quartered

1 green courgette, halved lengthways and crossways

1 yellow courgette, halved lengthways and crossways

10 large fresh mushrooms

Preparation: 30 minutes ✳ Cooking: 10 minutes ✳ Serves 4

✳ To make the marinade, in a large bowl, combine the vinegar, oil, soy sauce, mustard and honey and whisk until blended.

✳ Add the peppers, courgettes and mushrooms and toss to coat well. Cover, refrigerate and marinate for 15 minutes to 8 hours.

✳ Prepare a fire in an outdoor barbecue or preheat the grill. Place the vegetables on the grill and discard the marinade. Grill for 5 minutes. Turn and grill just until char marks appear, about 5 minutes more.

✳ To serve, divide amongst 4 individual plates.

Nutritional Analysis per Serving

Calories 84 (Kilojoules 350); Total fat 4g; Saturated fat 1g; Protein 3g; Cholesterol 0mg; Carbohydrates 9g; Sodium 110mg; Dietary fibre 2g; Calories from fat 41%

Spring Vegetable Sauté

1 teaspoon hazelnut oil

250 g (8 oz) sugar snap peas

½ fennel bulb, peeled and thinly sliced

2 carrots, peeled and thinly sliced

2 shallots, peeled and thinly sliced

¼ teaspoon salt

Preparation: 10 minutes ✳ Cooking: 8 minutes ✳ Serves 4

All vegetable oils contain the anti-oxidant vitamin E, but hazelnut oil has the most. Even the scant amount used here – ¼ teaspoon per serving – contains 4 per-cent of the recommended daily requirement.

✳ Coat a non-stick frying pan with non-stick cooking spray. Place over a medium heat and heat the hazelnut oil. Add the peas, fennel, carrots, shallots and salt and sauté, stirring frequently, until tender-crisp, 5–8 minutes.

✳ To serve, divide amongst 4 individual plates.

Nutritional Analysis per Serving

Calories 50 (Kilojoules 210); Total fat 1g; Saturated fat 0g; Protein 3g; Cholesterol 0mg; Carbohydrates 7g; Sodium 142mg; Dietary fibre 3g; Calories from fat 24%

1 aubergine, about 625 g (1¼ lb), cut
    into 2.5 cm (1 in) cubes
2 courgettes, cut into 2.5 cm (1 in)
    cubes
1 large onion, chopped
1 red pepper, seeded, cored and cut
    into 2.5 cm (1 in) cubes
1 green pepper, seeded, cored and
    cut into 2.5 cm (1 in) cubes
2 garlic cloves, very finely chopped
2 tomatoes, chopped
1 tablespoon chopped fresh thyme
1 tablespoon fresh basil
¼ teaspoon salt
¼ teaspoon ground black pepper

Nutrition Tip

✳ Red peppers are especially high
in vitamin C, having more than twice as
much as green peppers – themselves
a good source of the vitamin.

Ratatouille

Preparation: 30 minutes ✳ Cooking: 35 minutes ✳ Serves 4

*This version of the traditional French stew features summer vegetables.
Substitute other seasonal produce and make the dish all year round.*

✳ Preheat the grill. Coat a large baking sheet with non-stick
cooking spray. Spread the aubergine cubes on the prepared sheet
and lightly coat with cooking spray.

✳ Grill until golden, about 7 minutes, turning halfway through
the cooking time. Remove the baking sheet from the oven, add
the courgette, onion and peppers and lightly coat with non-stick
cooking spray.

✳ Grill until browned, turning halfway through the cooking
time, about 8 minutes more.

✳ Coat a large non-stick frying pan with non-stick cooking
spray and place over a medium heat. Add the garlic and sauté for
2 minutes.

✳ Add the tomatoes, thyme, basil, salt and pepper, reduce the
heat to low and simmer for 5 minutes.

✳ Add the vegetables to the tomato mixture and stir to mix
well. Cover and simmer until the liquid is reduced by half, about
10 minutes.

✳ To serve, divide amongst 4 individual plates.

Nutritional Analysis per Serving

Calories 72 (Kilojoules 304); Total fat 1g; Saturated fat 0g; Protein 4g;
Cholesterol 0mg; Carbohydrates 12g; Sodium 140mg; Dietary fibre 6g;
Calories from fat 17%

155g (5 oz) stone-ground
    yellow cornmeal

2 teaspoons baking powder

1 teaspoon chilli powder

½ teaspoon salt

375 g (12 oz) sweetcorn

3 tablespoons honey

250 ml (8 fl oz) buttermilk

3 tablespoons safflower oil

3 egg whites

60 g (2 oz) reduced fat Cheddar
    cheese

3 green chillies, seeded and chopped

Storage Tip

✳ Store this side dish wrapped in cling film in the refrigerator for up to 2 days.

Sweetcorn Pudding

Preparation: 20 minutes ✳ *Cooking: 40 minutes* ✳ *Serves 4*

This recipe makes four generous servings of this hearty side dish. Use it as an alternative to bread or rolls. Each serving fulfils both a grain and a vegetable requirement of a healthy daily diet.

✳ Preheat the oven to 180°C (350°F/Gas 4). Coat a 23 cm (9 in) round cake tin with non-stick cooking spray.

✳ In a large bowl, combine the cornmeal, baking powder, chilli powder and salt. Make a well in the centre.

✳ In another large bowl, using a wire whisk, combine the sweetcorn, honey, buttermilk, oil and egg whites. Add the cheese and chillies and stir to mix well.

✳ Pour the sweetcorn mixture into the well in the dry ingredients and stir until blended. Transfer to the prepared pan and bake until golden and a cocktail stick inserted in the centre comes out clean, about 30 minutes. Cool in the pan for 10 minutes before slicing.

✳ To serve, divide amongst 4 individual plates.

Nutritional Analysis per Serving

Calories 443 (Kilojoules 1,861); Total fat 13g; Saturated fat 3g; Protein 16g; Cholesterol 8mg; Carbohydrates 67g; Sodium 924mg; Dietary fibre 2g; Calories from fat 27%

3 large baking potatoes, about 750g
   (1½ lb), peeled

1 litre (1¾ pints) water

1 tablespoon white wine vinegar

2 egg whites

1 teaspoon paprika

½ teaspoon salt

Baked French Fries

Preparation: 35 minutes ✳ *Cooking: 40 minutes* ✳ *Serves 4*

✳ Slice the potatoes lengthways into matchsticks, about 0.5 cm (¼ in) thick. In a large bowl, combine the water, vinegar and potatoes. Set aside, uncovered, for 15 minutes at room temperature.

✳ Preheat the oven to 200°C (400°F/Gas 4). Coat a large baking sheet with non-stick cooking spray.

✳ In a small bowl, using an electric mixer on high speed, beat the egg whites until foamy.

✳ Place the potatoes on the prepared baking sheet in a single layer. Brush the tops and sides with the beaten egg whites and sprinkle with the paprika and salt. Bake, turning several times, until golden brown and crisp, about 40 minutes.

✳ To serve, divide amongst 4 individual plates.

Nutritional Analysis per Serving

Calories 149 (Kilojoules 633); Total fat 1g; Saturated fat 0g; Protein 5g; Cholesterol 0mg; Carbohydrates 32g; Sodium 290mg; Dietary fibre 2g; Calories from fat 3%

Rosemary Roasted Potatoes

Preparation: 10 minutes ✳ *Cooking: 1 hour* ✳ *Serves 4*

✳ Preheat the oven to 200°C (400°F/Gas 6). On a large baking sheet, spread out the potatoes and lightly coat the tops and sides with non-stick cooking spray. Sprinkle with the rosemary and pepper.

✳ Bake, turning every 15 minutes, until golden brown and tender in the middle, about 1 hour.

✳ To serve, divide amongst 4 individual plates.

Nutritional Analysis per Serving

Calories 142 (Kilojoules 600); Total fat 1g; Saturated fat 0g; Protein 4g; Cholesterol 0mg; Carbohydrates 32g; Sodium 13mg; Dietary fibre 2g; Calories from fat 3%

3 large baking potatoes, about 750 g
   (1½ lb), peeled and cut into
   5 cm (2 in) chunks

2 tablespoons chopped fresh rosemary

½ teaspoon ground black pepper

Garlic Mashed Potatoes

4 large baking potatoes, about 1 kg
    (2¼ lb), scrubbed and quartered

4 garlic cloves, peeled

1.5 litres (2½ pints) water

125 ml (4 fl oz) buttermilk

½ teaspoon ground black pepper

¼ teaspoon grated nutmeg

10 g (⅓ oz) fresh flat-leaf parsley,
    chopped

*Preparations: 15 minutes * Cooking: 15 minutes * Serves 4*

✳ In a large saucepan over a high heat, combine the potatoes, garlic and water. Bring to the boil, then reduce the heat to low, cover and simmer until the potatoes are tender when pierced with a fork, about 15 minutes. Drain, reserving 60 ml (2 fl oz) of the cooking water.

✳ In a large bowl, combine the potatoes and garlic, reserved cooking water, buttermilk, pepper and nutmeg. Using an electric mixer on high speed or a potato masher, mash until smooth, about 2 minutes by machine or 5 minutes by hand. Add the parsley and stir to mix well.

✳ To serve, divide amongst 4 individual plates.

Nutritional Analysis per Serving

Calories 203 (Kilojoules 860); Total fat 1g; Saturated fat 0g; Protein 7g; Cholesterol 1mg; Carbohydrates 45g; Sodium 36mg; Dietary fibre 4g; Calories from fat 3%

Nutrition Tip

✳ Substituting buttermilk for the traditional whole milk and butter gives these mashed potatoes plenty of taste but far fewer fat grams and calories. Leaving the skins increases the vitamins and fibre and provides an appealing texture.

Orzo with Shallots and Herbs

2 litres (3½ pints) water

250 g (8 oz) dried orzo

3 shallots, peeled and chopped

125 ml (4 fl oz) Chicken Stock
    (recipe on page 206) or canned
    reduced sodium chicken broth

1 tablespoon chopped fresh basil

1 tablespoon chopped fresh oregano

1 tablespoon chopped fresh tarragon

¼ teaspoon salt

¼ teaspoon ground black pepper

*Preparation: 20 minutes * Cooking: 10 minutes * Serves 4*

✳ In a large saucepan over a high heat, bring the water to the boil. Add the orzo and shallots and cook until the orzo is tender, about 10 minutes. Drain.

✳ In a large bowl, combine the stock or broth, basil, oregano, tarragon, salt and pepper. Add the orzo and shallots and stir to mix well.

✳ To serve, divide amongst 4 individual plates. Serve hot or cold.

Nutritional Analysis per Serving

Calories 222 (Kilojoules 946); Total fat 1g; Saturated fat 0g; Protein 8g; Cholesterol 0mg; Carbohydrates 48g; Sodium 156mg; Dietary fibre 2g; Calories from fat 5%

1.5 kg (3 lb) chicken pieces,
    including necks and backs if desired

3 onions, chopped

4 carrots, peeled and chopped

4 celery stalks with leaves, chopped

2 fresh flat-leaf parsley sprigs

5 fresh thyme sprigs

2 bay leaves

1 teaspoon salt

8 whole black peppercorns

3 litres (5¼ pints) water

Cooking Tip

✳ Substitute a whole roast bird from which you have eaten half the meat for the chicken pieces, if desired.

Chicken Stock

Preparation: 15 minutes ✳ *Cooking: 2 hours 40 minutes* ✳ *Makes 3 qt (3 l)*

Home-made chicken stock is indispensable as a foundation for soups, stews and chowders. When you make your own, you can season the stock with your favourite herbs and spices and add the amount of sodium that best suits your dietary needs. This is the kind of cooking you can do while busy with other tasks around the house.

✳ In a large saucepan over a high heat, combine the chicken pieces, onions, carrots, celery, parsley, thyme, bay leaves, salt, peppercorns and water. Increase the heat to high and bring to the boil. Reduce the heat to medium-high and boil, uncovered, for 15 minutes. Using kitchen paper, skim the foam that rises to the surface. Reduce the heat to low, cover and simmer for 2 hours, skimming the surface as needed. Remove from the heat and cool 20 minutes.

✳ Strain the stock through a fine-mesh sieve over a large bowl to remove the solids, pressing hard on the chicken and vegetables to extract their full flavour. Cover and refrigerate for at least 8 hours.

✳ Using kitchen paper, skim the congealed fat from the cold stock. Transfer to airtight containers and refrigerate for up to 3 days or freeze for up to 3 months. For nutritional analysis, one serving is 250ml (8fl oz).

Nutritional Analysis per Serving

Calories 25 (Kilojoules 106); Total fat 2g; Saturated fat 1g; Protein 3g;
Cholesterol 0mg; Carbohydrates 2g; Sodium 277mg; Dietary fibre 0g;
Calories from fat 72%

5 carrots, peeled and chopped

5 celery stalks, with leaves, chopped

2 onions, quartered

15 g (½ oz) fresh flat-leaf parsley,
chopped

5 fresh thyme sprigs

2 fresh oregano sprigs

10 whole black peppercorns

1 dried red chilli pepper, halved

4 litres (7 pints) water

Storage Tip

✳ Make the stock ahead and store in air-tight containers such as sealable plastic freezer bags or bottles. For convenience, freeze the stock in ice-cube trays and use the frozen cubes as necessary. The stock keeps in the refrigerator for up to 3 days or in the freezer for up to 3 months.

Vegetable Stock

Preparation: 20 minutes ✳ Cooking: 1 hour ✳ Makes 4 qt (4 l)

This vegetable stock is a wonderful non-fat base for soups, stews and sauces. Also, use it whenever water is called for in rice and whole-grain dishes to add flavour and nutrients.

✳ In a large saucepan over a high heat, combine the carrots, celery, onions, parsley, thyme, oregano, peppercorns, chilli pepper and water. Bring to the boil, then reduce the heat to medium and simmer, covered, for 1 hour. Remove from the heat and cool 20 minutes.

✳ Strain the stock through a fine-mesh sieve over a large bowl to remove the solids, pressing hard on the vegetables to extract their full flavour. Transfer to airtight containers and refrigerate for up to 3 days or freeze for up to 3 months. For nutritional analysis, one serving is 250 ml (8 fl oz).

Nutritional Analysis per Serving

Calories 12 (Kilojoules 50); Total fat 0g; Saturated fat 0g; Protein 0g; Cholesterol 0mg; Carbohydrates 3g; Sodium 15mg; Dietary fibre 1g; Calories from fat 0%

2 teaspoons olive oil

1 garlic clove, very finely chopped

2 teaspoons grated fresh root ginger

⅛ teaspoon crushed red pepper flakes

220 g (7 oz) basmati rice

45 g (1½ oz) flaked almonds

1 bay leaf

500ml (16 fl oz) Chicken
  Stock (recipe on page 206) or
  canned reduced sodium chicken
  broth

½ teaspoon salt

Spicy Rice Pilaff

Preparation: 15 minutes ✳ Cooking: 25 minutes ✳ Serves 4

✳ In a medium saucepan over a medium heat, heat the oil. Add the garlic, ginger and red pepper flakes and sauté, stirring frequently, for 2 minutes. Add the rice, almonds and bay leaf and sauté, stirring frequently, until the rice is golden, about 3 minutes more. Add the stock or broth and salt, increase the heat to medium-high and bring to the boil.

✳ Reduce the heat to low, cover and simmer until the liquid is absorbed, about 20 minutes.

✳ To serve, remove and discard the bay leaf, fluff with a fork and divide amongst 4 individual plates.

Nutritional Analysis per Serving

Calories 286 (Kilojoules 1,191); Total fat 9g; Saturated fat 1g; Protein 7g; Cholesterol 0mg; Carbohydrates 45g; Sodium 654mg; Dietary fibre 1g; Calories from fat 27%

Wild Rice with Mixed Dried Fruit

Preparation: 20 minutes ✳ Cooking: 1 hour 10 minutes ✳ Serves 4

✳ In a medium saucepan over a medium heat, heat the oil. Add the garlic and celery and sauté for 2 minutes. Add the rice and mixed dried fruit and sauté for 2 minutes more.

✳ Add the stock or broth, thyme, sage and pepper, increase the heat to medium-high and bring to the boil.

✳ Reduce the heat to low, cover and simmer, stirring occasionally, for 1 hour. Uncover and simmer until the liquid is absorbed, about 5 minutes more.

✳ To serve, fluff with a fork and divide amongst 4 individual plates.

Nutritional Analysis per Serving

Calories 208 (Kilojoules 885); Total fat 3g; Saturated fat 0g; Protein 3g; Cholesterol 0mg; Carbohydrates 46g; Sodium 354mg; Dietary fibre 3g; Calories from fat 11%

2 teaspoons vegetable oil

2 garlic cloves, very finely chopped

1 celery stalk, chopped

140 g (4½ oz) wild rice

90 g (3 oz) chopped mixed dried
  fruit, such as prunes, pears, apples
  and apricots

600 ml (1 pint) Chicken Stock (recipe
  on page 206) or canned reduced
  sodium chicken broth

2 tablespoons chopped fresh thyme

1 tablespoon chopped fresh sage

¼ teaspoon ground black pepper

15 g (½ oz) margarine

1 large onion, chopped

4 celery stalks, chopped

1 tart apple, such as Granny Smith,
    peeled, cored and cubed

10 g (⅓ oz) fresh flat-leaf parsley,
    chopped

2 tablespoons chopped fresh oregano

2 teaspoons chopped fresh sage

1 tablespoon chopped fresh rosemary

¼ teaspoon ground black pepper

315 g (10 oz) wholemeal bread cubes,
    lightly toasted

500 ml (16 fl oz) Chicken Stock
    (recipe on page 206) or canned
    reduced sodium chicken broth

Bread and Apple Dressing

*Preparation: 25 minutes * Cooking: 30 minutes * Serves 4*

✳ Preheat the oven to 180°C (350°F/Gas 4). Coat a 2 litre (3½ pint) ovenproof dish with non-stick cooking spray.

✳ In a large non-stick frying pan over a medium heat, melt the margarine. Add the onion, celery and apple and sauté, stirring frequently, for 5 minutes. Add the parsley, oregano, sage, rosemary and pepper and stir to mix well.

✳ Transfer the mixture to a large bowl and add the bread cubes and stock or broth. Toss to mix well. Pour into the prepared dish and bake, uncovered, until golden brown and the liquid is absorbed, about 25 minutes. To serve, divide amongst 4 individual plates.

Nutritional Analysis per Serving

Calories 222 (Kilojoules 941); Total fat 8g; Saturated fat 1g; Protein 8g; Cholesterol 0mg; Carbohydrates 38g; Sodium 479mg; Dietary fibre 6g; Calories from fat 21%

2 teaspoons olive oil

2 shallots, peeled and minced

2 celery stalks, diced

220 g (7 oz) brown rice

560 ml (18 fl oz) Chicken Stock
    (recipe on page 206) or canned
    reduced sodium chicken broth

90 g (3 oz) sultanas

2 tablespoons chopped fresh rosemary

¼ teaspoon salt

¼ teaspoon ground black pepper

Rice, Raisin and Rosemary Dressing

*Preparation: 20 minutes * Cooking: 1 hour * Serves 4*

✳ Preheat the oven to 180°C (350°F/Gas 4). Coat a 2 litre (3½ pint) ovenproof dish with non-stick cooking spray.

✳ In a medium saucepan over a medium heat, heat the oil. Add the shallots and celery and sauté, stirring often for 3 minutes. Add the rice and sauté until golden, about 3 minutes more. Add the stock or broth, raisins, rosemary, salt and pepper and bring to the boil. Reduce the heat to low, cover and simmer for 15 minutes.

✳ Transfer to the prepared dish and bake, uncovered, until golden, about 40 minutes. To serve, divide amongst 4 individual plates.

Nutritional Analysis per Serving

Calories 284 (Kilojoules 1,204); Total fat 4g; Saturated fat 1g; Protein 5g; Cholesterol 0mg; Carbohydrates 62g; Sodium 420mg; Dietary fibre 2g; Calories from fat 12%

875 ml (28 fl oz) water

2 tablespoons lemon juice

4 large tart apples such as
Granny Smith

60 g (2 oz) dried cranberries

3 tablespoons sugar

1 cinnamon stick, about 7.5 cm (3 in)
long

1 teaspoon finely grated lemon rind

Storage Tip

✳ To chill the dessert, cool at room temperature for 20 minutes. Transfer to an airtight container and refrigerate for up to 4 days. For the best results, allow the compôte to sit at room temperature for 15 minutes before serving.

Cranberry Apple Sauce

Preparation: 15 minutes ✳ Cooking: 15 minutes ✳ Serves 4

This dessert is delicious served hot or cold paired with grilled chicken, pork and game dishes. It makes a great breakfast side dish, too.

✳ In a medium bowl, combine 500 ml (16 fl oz) of the water and 1 tablespoon of the lemon juice.

✳ Peel and core the apples and slice into 2.5 cm (1 in) chunks, dropping the chunks into the water and lemon mixture to prevent browning.

✳ In a medium saucepan over a medium-high heat, combine the remaining water and lemon juice and the cranberries, sugar and cinnamon stick and bring to the boil.

✳ Drain the apples, discard the water and add the apples to the saucepan. Reduce the heat to low and simmer, partially covered, until the apples are tender when pierced with a fork but still whole, about 5 minutes. Using a slotted spoon, transfer the apples and cranberries to a serving bowl.

✳ Increase the heat to high and bring the remaining liquid and cinnamon stick to the boil. Boil until the liquid is reduced by a third. Remove from the heat, remove and discard the cinnamon stick and stir in the lemon rind.

✳ Pour the syrup over the apples and cranberries and stir, mashing slightly.

✳ To serve, divide amongst 4 individual bowls.

Nutritional Analysis per Serving

Calories 121 (Kilojoules 520); Total fat 0g; Saturated fat 0g; Protein 0g; Cholesterol 0mg; Carbohydrates 32g; Sodium 5mg; Dietary fibre 4g; Calories from fat 2%

315 g (10 oz) unbleached plain flour

250 g (8 oz) sugar

60 g (2 oz) almonds, toasted

¾ teaspoon bicarbonate of soda

¼ teaspoon salt

2 eggs

2 egg whites

1 teaspoon vanilla essence

½ teaspoon almond essence

Cooking Tip

✳ To toast almonds, or any kind of shelled nut, spread on a baking sheet and toast in a 180°C (350°F/Gas 4) oven until lightly golden, 4–5 minutes, tossing the nuts halfway through the cooking time.

Almond Biscotti

Preparation: 20 minutes ✳ *Cooking: 55 minutes* ✳ *Serves 18*

These crisp Italian biscuits – the name means "twice baked" – are wonderful for dipping into a hot drink. Serve them as a low fat dessert, breakfast pastry or low fat snack. They're an excellent choice for making ahead and having on hand for unexpected guests as they will keep in an airtight container for up to a week. The taste actually improves after a day or two of storage.

✳ Preheat the oven to 170°C (325°F/Gas 3). Coat a baking sheet with non-stick cooking spray.

✳ In a large bowl, combine the flour, sugar, almonds, bicarbonate of soda and salt. In a medium bowl, whisk together the eggs, egg whites, and vanilla and almond essences. Add the egg mixture to the dry ingredients and stir until just blended. Turn the dough on to a well floured work surface and shape into a smooth ball. Shape into a 25 cm (10 in) log and place on the prepared baking sheet. Bake until a cocktail stick inserted in the centre comes out clean, 30–35 minutes. Cool for 5 minutes.

✳ Reduce the oven to 150°C (300°F/Gas 1). Place the log on a work surface and slice into 18 pieces. Arrange the slices on the baking sheet and bake, turning once about halfway through, until golden brown, about 20 minutes. Cool until crisp.

✳ Store in an airtight container at room temperature for up to 1 week. One serving is one biscuit.

Nutritional Analysis per Serving

Calories 146 (Kilojoules 617); Total fat 3g; Saturated fat 0g; Protein 3g; Cholesterol 26mg; Carbohydrates 28g; Sodium 90mg; Dietary fibre 1g; Calories from fat 18%

315 g (10 oz) unbleached plain flour

90 g (3 oz) rolled oats

90 g (3 oz) pecans, chopped and
  lightly toasted

1 teaspoon bicarbonate of soda

¼ teaspoon salt

250 g (8 oz) low fat soft cheese

2 tablespoons margarine

125 g (4 oz) sugar

125 ml (4 fl oz) orange juice

2 tablespoons virtually no fat vanilla
  yogurt

1 egg

1 egg white

1 tablespoon finely grated orange rind

1 teaspoon vanilla essence

185 g (6 oz) icing sugar

Orange Pecan Cookies

Preparation: 20 minutes ✳ Cooking: 15 minutes ✳ Serves 20

*A refreshing orange flavour permeates this twist on oatmeal drop cookies.
I recommend you add these to your baking repertoire. While they are
sweet enough to satisfy even my sugar cravings, the use of orange juice,
low fat soft cheese and yogurt, rather than lots of sugar and butter, keeps
them relatively low calorie and low fat.*

✳ Preheat the oven to 180°C (350°F/Gas 4). Coat 2 large
baking sheets with non stick cooking spray.

✳ In a medium bowl, combine the flour, oats, pecans,
bicarbonate of soda and salt. In a food processor with the metal
blade or in a large bowl, combine the cheese, margarine
and sugar. Process or stir until smooth. Add half of the orange
juice, the yogurt, egg, egg white, orange rind and vanilla.
Process or stir until smooth. Gradually add the flour mixture
and process or stir until just blended.

✳ Drop about 60 rounded tablespoons on to the prepared baking
sheets. Bake until golden at the edges, about 15 minutes.

✳ To make the glaze, in a small bowl, combine the remaining
orange juice and the icing sugar and whisk until smooth. Using a
pastry brush, coat the warm cookies with the glaze.

✳ Store in an airtight container at room temperature for up to
one week. One serving is 3 cookies.

Nutritional Analysis per Serving

Calories 174 (Kilojoules 734); Total fat 6g; Saturated fat 1g; Protein 5g;
Cholesterol 12mg; Carbohydrates 26g; Sodium 180mg; Dietary fibre 1g;
Calories from fat 32%

Pears with Chocolate Sauce

4 firm Anjou or Bosc pears, peeled,
  halved and cored

2 tablespoons lemon juice

125 ml (4 fl oz) boiling water

3 tablespoons sugar

2 tablespoons light corn syrup

Chocolate Sauce

155 g (5 oz) sugar

125 ml (4 fl oz) skimmed milk

20 g (⅔ oz) cocoa

1½ tablespoons cornflour

1 teaspoon vanilla essence

*Preparation: 25 minutes * Cooking: 40 minutes * Serves 4*

Choose slightly underripe, firm pears for this autumn dessert as overly soft fruit may turn mushy during cooking. Pears are a good source of vitamins A and C. In addition to the preparation time, allow at least 20 minutes for the pears to chill before serving.

✳ Preheat the oven to 180°C (350°F/Gas 4).

✳ In a 23 x 13 x 5 cm (13 x 9 x 2in) ovenproof dish, arrange the pears, cut side down, and top with the lemon juice.

✳ In a small bowl, combine the water, sugar and corn syrup and stir to mix well. Pour over the pears. Cover the dish with aluminium foil and bake until the pears are tender when pierced with a fork, 25–35 minutes. Cool in the pan for 10 minutes.

✳ Using a slotted spoon, transfer the pears to a container, cover and refrigerate for 20 minutes to 8 hours. Discard the syrup.

✳ To serve, slice each pear half lengthways into thin slices, without cutting all the way through the stem end. Place 2 halves on each dessert plate and press down gently to form fans. Top each with 1 tablespoon of the chocolate sauce.

Chocolate Sauce

✳ In a small saucepan over a medium heat, combine the sugar, milk, cocoa and cornflour. Simmer, stirring constantly with a wire whisk, until the mixture thickens, about 5 minutes. Remove from the heat and stir in the vanilla. Store in an airtight container in the refrigerator for up to one week. One serving is 1 tablespoon.

Nutritional Analysis per Serving

Calories 348 (Kilojoules 1,480); Total fat 2g; Saturated fat 1g; Protein 3g; Cholesterol 1mg; Carbohydrates 87g; Sodium 90mg; Dietary fibre 4g; Calories from fat 4%

60 g (2 oz) sugar

250 ml (8 fl oz) water

1 vanilla pod, split lengthways

185 g (6 oz) peeled, cantaloupe, cubed

185 g (6 oz) peeled honeydew melon, cubed

125 g (4 oz) blueberries

10 g (6 oz) fresh mint, chopped

4 fresh mint sprigs

Shopping Tip

You'll find whole vanilla pods in jars in the spice section of most markets. If you can't find them, substitute 1 teaspoon vanilla essence. Stir it into the cooked syrup.

Melon and Blueberries in Sauce

Preparation: 20 minutes ✱ Cooking: 35 minutes ✱ Serves 4

In addition to the preparation and cooking times, you'll need to allow 2 hours for chilling before serving. Melons, blueberries and mint – summertime favourites – are all rich in vitamins A and C, so enjoy this colourful dessert knowing it's both good and good for you.

✱ To make the syrup, in a small saucepan over a medium heat, dissolve the sugar in the water. Scrape the seeds from the vanilla pod and add the seeds and pod to the pan. Reduce the heat to low and simmer, stirring constantly, until the syrup is hot, about 3 minutes. Remove from the heat and let steep for 30 minutes.

✱ Strain the syrup through a fine-mesh sieve and discard the vanilla pod.

✱ In a large bowl, combine the melon cubes, blueberries and chopped mint. Add the strained syrup and toss to coat well. Cover and refrigerate for at least 2 hours.

✱ To serve, divide amongst 4 individual dessert dishes and top with the mint sprigs. Serve chilled or at room temperature.

Nutritional Analysis per Serving

Calories 91 (Kilojoules 389); Total fat 0g; Saturated fat 0g; Protein 1g; Cholesterol 0mg; Carbohydrates 23g; Sodium 21mg; Dietary fibre 1g; Calories from fat 2%

Baked Apples

4 tart apples, such as Granny Smith,
  peeled and cored

2 tablespoons lemon juice

2 tablespoons chopped almonds

1 tablespoon firmly packed
  brown sugar

2 teaspoons margarine

½ teaspoon ground cinnamon

½ teaspoon vanilla essence

4 sheets frozen filo pastry, thawed,
  unfolded and stacked

1 egg white

2 tablespoons flaked almonds

2 teaspoons sugar

*Preparation: 25 minutes * Cooking: 40 minutes * Serves 4*

Wrapped apples can be prepared up to two days ahead. Just assemble, cover with cling film and refrigerate, then bake before serving. Frozen filo pastry can be thawed, wrapped airtight, in the refrigerator for 8 hours or overnight. To prevent the pastry sheets from drying out and becoming brittle, cover them with cling film or greaseproof paper and a damp towel while you prepare the apples.

✳ Preheat the oven to 180°C (350°F/Gas 4). Coat a shallow non-metallic dish with non-stick cooking spray. Brush the apples with the lemon juice.

✳ In a small bowl, mix together the chopped almonds, brown sugar, margarine, cinnamon and vanilla. Spoon an equal amount of the mixture into the hollowed-out cores of each apple.

✳ Using a sharp knife, cut the stacked filo sheets into quarters. Place an apple, base side down, on to the centre of each stack and bring up the edges and tuck the ends into the hollowed-out core.

✳ Place the wrapped apples, seam side down, in the prepared dish and brush with the egg white. Top with the sliced almonds and sprinkle with the sugar. Bake until the pastry is golden, 35–40 minutes.

✳ To serve, divide amongst 4 individual dessert plates.

Nutritional Analysis per Serving

Calories 244 (Kilojoules 1024); Total fat 10g; Saturated fat 1g; Protein 7g; Cholesterol 0mg; Carbohydrates 33g; Sodium 132mg; Dietary fibre 3g; Calories from fat 37%

315 g (10 oz) raspberries

250 ml (8 fl oz) skimmed milk

60 g (2 oz) sugar

4 fresh mint sprigs

Raspberry Sherbet

Preparation: 20 minutes ✳ Chilling: 2 hours ✳ Serves 4

✳ In a blender, combine the raspberries, milk and sugar and process until smooth.

✳ Pour into a 33 x 23 x 5 cm (13 x 9 x 2 in) freezerproof dish. Cover and freeze until firm, about 2 hours.

✳ Return the sherbet to the blender in batches and process until smooth. Freeze in the dish until ready to serve.

✳ To serve, divide amongst 4 individual dessert dishes. Garnish each with a mint sprig.

Nutritional Analysis per Serving

Calories 99 (Kilojoules 425); Total fat 1g; Saturated fat 0g; Protein 3g; Cholesterol 1mg; Carbohydrates 23g; Sodium 37mg; Dietary fibre 2g; Calories from fat 3%

375 ml (12 fl oz) orange juice

315 g (10 oz) blueberries

375 ml (12 fl oz) buttermilk

60 g (2 oz) sugar

40 ml (2 fl oz) lemon juice

1 teaspoon finely grated lemon rind

8 fresh mint sprigs

Lemon Blueberry Ice Milk

Preparation: 20 minutes ✳ Chilling: 2 hours ✳ Serves 8

✳ In a blender, combine the orange juice, 250 g (8 oz) of blueberries, the buttermilk, sugar and lemon juice and rind and process until smooth.

✳ Pour into a 33 x 13 x 2 cm (13 x 9 x 2 in) freezerproof dish. Cover and freeze until firm, about 2 hours.

✳ Return the ice milk to the blender in batches and process until smooth. Freeze in the dish until ready to serve.

✳ To serve, divide amongst 8 individual dessert dishes. Top each with an equal amount of the remaining berries. Garnish each with a mint sprig.

Nutritional Analysis per Serving

Calories 76 (Kilojoules 323); Total fat 1g; Saturated fat 0g; Protein 2g; Cholesterol 1mg; Carbohydrates 17g; Sodium 33mg; Dietary fibre 1g; Calories from fat 4%

90 g (3 oz) sifted cake flour

1 teaspoon baking powder

⅛ teaspoon salt

3 eggs, separated

250 g (8 oz) sugar

2 teaspoons vanilla essence

60 ml (2 fl oz) water

2 egg whites

Chocolate Orange Icing

375 g (12 oz) icing sugar, sifted

30 g (1 oz) cocoa

60 ml (2 fl oz) boiling water

30 g (1 oz) margarine

½ teaspoon vanilla essence

½ teaspoon orange essence

Cooking Tip

✳ For a different-flavoured icing, substitute almond, lemon or additional vanilla essence for the orange essence.

Sponge Cake with Chocolate Orange Icing

Preparation: 35 minutes ✳ *Cooking: 20 minutes* ✳ *Serves 16*

✳ Preheat the oven to 180°C (350°F/Gas 4). Coat a 33 x 23 x 5 cm (13 x 9 x 2 in) baking tin with non-stick cooking spray.

✳ In a small bowl, combine the flour, baking powder and salt.

✳ In a large bowl, using an electric mixer on high speed, beat the 3 egg yolks for 1 minute. With the mixer on high speed, gradually beat in 185 g (6 oz) of the sugar. Continue beating on high speed until the mixture is thick and the yolks are pale, about 3 minutes.

✳ With the mixer on medium speed, beat in the vanilla and water. With the mixer on low speed, gradually add the dry ingredients and beat until blended.

✳ In another large bowl, using an electric mixer on high speed and clean beaters, beat the 5 egg whites until foamy. Continuing to beat on high speed, gradually add the remaining sugar until stiff peaks form.

✳ Stir 125 ml (1 fl oz) of the egg white mixture into the egg yolk and flour mixture. Fold in the remaining egg whites.

✳ Pour into the prepared tin and bake until the cake springs back when pressed in the centre, about 20 minutes. Cool in the tin. When the cake is cool, spread the top with the Chocolate Orange Icing.

✳ To serve, slice into 16 pieces and divide among individual dessert plates. Store wrapped in cling film in the refrigerator for up to 3 days.

Chocolate Orange Icing

✳ In a large bowl, combine the icing sugar, cocoa, water, margarine and essences. Using an electric mixer on high speed, beat until smooth.

Nutritional Analysis per Serving

Calories 211 (Kilojoules 895); Total fat 3g; Saturated fat 1g; Protein 3g; Cholesterol 45mg; Carbohydrates 46g; Sodium 102mg; Dietary fibre 0g; Calories from fat 14%

2 cantaloupe melons, halved
   and seeded
16 fl oz (500 ml) Rasperry Sherbet
   (recipe on page 224)
4 egg whites
60 g (2 oz) sugar
1 teaspoon vanilla essence (essence)

Nutrition Tip

✳ Cantaloupe is an outstanding source
of vitamins A and C. It also offers a lot of
the anti-oxidant beta-carotene, along with
ample fibre and B vitamins.

Meringue-Topped Cantaloupe

Preparation: 25 minutes ✳ *Cooking: 25 minutes* ✳ *Serves 4*

*Meringues must be fully cooked to eliminate the risks associated with
raw eggs. They will appear golden brown on top and completely set in
the middle. Store leftover meringues in an airtight container at room
temperature for up to 3 days.*

✳ Preheat the oven to 150°C (300°F/Gas 10). Coat a large
baking sheet with non-stick cooking spray.

✳ Using a melon baller, make balls from the 4 cantaloupe
halves, reserving the shells. Slice the base of each shell so that it
stands upright.

✳ In a large bowl, using an electric mixer on high speed, beat
the egg whites until soft peaks form. While continuing to beat on
high speed, gradually add the sugar until stiff peaks form. Gently
fold in the vanilla.

✳ Spoon the meringue on to the prepared baking sheet, forming
4 rounds of the same diameter as the cantaloupe shells. Bake
until golden brown and set in the centre, 20–25 minutes.

✳ To serve, place the cantaloupe shells on 4 individual plates, place
an equal amount of the melon balls and sherbet into each shell.
Top each with a meringue.

Nutritional Analysis per Serving

**Calories 299 (Kilojoules 1,255); Total fat 2g; Saturated fat 0g; Protein 10g;
Cholesterol 2mg; Carbohydrates 68g; Sodium 148mg; Dietary fibre 5g;
Calories from fat 6%**

Honey Mint Fruit Compôte

Preparation: 15 minutes ✳ *Chilling: 30 minutes* ✳ *Serves 4*

2 peaches or nectarines, peeled,
   stoned and sliced
125 g (4 oz) blueberries
125 g (4 oz) strawberries
185 g (6 oz) cantaloupe
   melon chunks
185 g (6 oz) honeydew or
   watermelon chunks
1 kiwifruit, peeled and sliced
2 tablespoons honey
40 ml (2 fl oz) orange juice
3 tablespoons chopped fresh mint
1 tablespoon lemon juice

✳ In a large bowl, combine the peaches or nectarines, blueberries, strawberries, cantaloupe, honeydew or watermelon and kiwifruit. In a small bowl, whisk together the honey, orange juice, mint and lemon juice.

✳ Spoon the honey mixture over the fruit, cover with cling film and refrigerate to allow the flavours to marry, at least 30 minutes.

✳ To serve, divide amongst 4 individual bowls. Serve chilled.

📝 *Nutritional Analysis per Serving*

Calories 96 (Kilojoules 407); Total fat 1g; Saturated fat 0g; Protein 2g; Cholesterol 0mg; Carbohydrates 23g; Sodium 25mg; Dietary fibre 3g; Calories from fat 3%

Pumpkin Spice Bread

Preparation: 20 minutes ✳ *Cooking: 1 hour* ✳ *Serves 8*

390 g (12½ oz) unbleached plain flour
2 teaspoons baking powder
½ teaspoon bicarbonate of soda
1½ teaspoons ground cinnamon
¼ teaspoon grated nutmeg
¼ teaspoon ground cloves
¼ teaspoon salt
60 g (2 oz) margarine
185 g (6 oz) sugar
105 g (3½ oz) brown sugar
2 eggs
1 egg white
470 g (15 oz) pumpkin purée
90 g (3 oz) plus 2 tablespoons
   virtually no fat plain yogurt

✳ Preheat the oven to 180°C (350°F/Gas 4). Coat a 23 x 13 cm (9 x 5 in) loaf tin with non-stick cooking spray.

✳ In a medium bowl, combine the flour, baking powder, baking soda, cinnamon, nutmeg, cloves and salt. In a large bowl, using an electric mixer or by hand, beat the margarine and sugars until creamy. Add the eggs and egg white and beat until blended. Add the pumpkin and yogurt and beat until smooth. Gradually add the flour mixture and beat until blended.

✳ Pour the mixture into the prepared loaf tin and bake until a cocktail stick inserted in the centre comes out clean, about 1 hour. Cool in the tin for 10 minutes.

✳ To serve, cut into 8 slices and place on individual plates. Store in an airtight container at room temperature for up to 2 days.

📝 *Nutritional Analysis per Serving*

Calories 400 (Kilojoules 1,692); Total fat 9g; Saturated fat 2g; Protein 8g; Cholesterol 60mg; Carbohydrates 78g; Sodium 386mg; Dietary fibre 2g; Calories from fat 20%

375 g (12 oz) skimmed milk

60 g (2 oz) plus 2 tablespoons
   sugar

2 teaspoons finely grated orange rind

½ teaspoon finely grated lemon rind

1 teaspoon vanilla essence

¼ teaspoon salt

4 egg yolks

Raspberry Sauce

315 g (10 oz) raspberries

2 tablespoons icing sugar

2 tablespoons cold water

2 teaspoons cornflour

Orange Custard with Raspberry Sauce

Preparation: 20 minutes ✳ Cooking: 1 hour 10 minutes ✳ Serves 4

You need to do some advance planning to serve this dessert because it takes over an hour to cook and needs another hour to chill. However, the preparation is fairly quick and the taste worth the effort. This custard is a good choice for a dinner party as it can be done ahead and the presentation will impress your guests.

✳ Preheat the oven to 170°C (325°F/Gas 3).

✳ In a medium bowl, combine the milk, sugar, orange and lemon rinds, vanilla, salt and egg yolks and whisk until blended.

✳ Divide amongst four 185 ml (6 fl oz) custard cups. Place the cups in a shallow ovenproof dish and add enough hot water to reach 2.5 cm (1 in) up the sides of the cups.

✳ Bake until a knife inserted in the centre comes out clean (the centre will still jiggle a little), 1 hour 10 minutes. Cool completely before serving, about 1 hour.

✳ To serve, top each custard with an equal amount of the Raspberry Sauce.

Raspberry Sauce

✳ Press the raspberries through a fine mesh sieve into a small saucepan to remove the seeds. Place the pan with the resulting purée and juice over a medium heat, add the icing sugar and simmer for 2 minutes. In a small jar, combine the water and cornflour and shake to mix well. Add to the raspberries and simmer, stirring frequently, until the sauce has thickened, about 3 minutes. Remove from the heat and cool before serving. One serving is 3 tablespoons.

Nutritional Analysis per Serving

Calories 247 (Kilojoules 1049); Total fat 6g; Saturated fat 2g; Protein 7g; Cholesterol 203mg; Carbohydrates 44g; Sodium 185mg; Dietary fibre 2g; Calories from fat 21%

Banana Cheesecake

45 g (1½ oz) plus 2 tablespoons
digestive biscuit crumbs

2 tablespoons plus 125 g (4 oz) sugar

30 g (1 oz) margarine, melted

4 large bananas, mashed

250 g (8 oz) low fat soft cheese

125 g (4 oz) low fat cottage cheese

1 egg

2 teaspoons vanilla essence

½ teaspoon sweetened cocoa powder

8 strawberries

8 fresh mint sprigs

*Preparation: 25 minutes * Cooking: 1 hour * Serves 8*

In addition to the preparation and cooking times, allow at least 1¼ hours for the cake to cool before serving. Ask your guests what the secret ingredient is in this dessert and few will guess that it's cottage cheese! The bananas and cottage cheese replace most of the cream cheese – and its fat – found in traditional cheesecakes. Bananas also supply vitamins, niacine and potassium.

✱ Preheat the oven to 150°C (300°F/Gas 1). Coat the base and sides of a 23 cm (9 in) spring-form pan with non-stick cooking spray.

✱ To make the base, in a medium bowl, combine the digestive biscuit crumbs, 2 tablespoons sugar and margarine and stir to mix well. Lightly press the mixture into the base of the prepared pan.

✱ To make the filling, in a food processor with the metal blade or in a blender, combine the bananas, soft cheese, cottage cheese, egg, vanilla and 125 g (4 oz) sugar and process until smooth.

✱ Pour the filling over the base and bake until the centre is set, about 1 hour. Turn off the oven, prop open the oven door and leave the cheesecake in the oven to cool for 15 minutes. Remove the cake from the oven and cool completely in the pan, about 1 hour.

✱ To serve, release the cake from the pan, sprinkle the top with the cocoa, slice into 8 wedges and divide amongst individual dessert plates. Garnish each wedge with a strawberry and a mint sprig. Store covered in the refrigerator for up to 4 days.

Nutritional Analysis per Serving

Calories 265 (Kilojoules 1,117); Total fat 8g; Saturated fat 2g; Protein 9g; Cholesterol 34mg; Carbohydrates 42g; Sodium 250mg; Dietary fibre 1g; Calories from fat 27%

45 g (1½ oz) plus 2 tablespoons
    digestive biscuit crumbs

2 tablespoons plus 185 g (6 oz) sugar

30 g (1 oz) margarine, melted

500 g (1 lb) ricotta cheese

250 g (8 oz) low fat soft cream cheese

1 egg

1½ teaspoons vanilla essence

30 g (1 oz) cocoa

3 tablespoons plain flour

45 g (1½ oz) plain chocolate, melted
    and cooled

125 g (4 oz) virtually no fat
    vanilla yogurt

3 tablespoons soured cream

7 g (¼ oz) plain chocolate, grated

Chocolate Cheesecake

Preparation: 25 minutes ✳ Cooking: 1 hour ✳ Serves 8

In addition to the preparation and cooking times, allow at least 1¼ hours for the cake to cool before serving. This cake satisfies even the most serious "chocoholic". The chocolate makes the cake sweeter than plain versions, but it is still not so sweet that fans of more tangy cheesecakes won't enjoy it.

✳ Preheat the oven to 150°C (300°F/Gas 1). Coat the base and sides of a 23 cm (9 in) spring-form pan with non-stick cooking spray.

✳ To make the base, in a medium bowl, combine the digestive biscuit crumbs, 2 tablespoons sugar and margarine and stir to mix well. Lightly press the mixture into the base of the prepared pan.

✳ To make the filling, in a food processor with the metal blade or in a blender, combine the ricotta, soft cheese and 185 g (6 oz) sugar and process until smooth. Add the egg and vanilla and process until blended. Gradually add the cocoa, flour and melted chocolate and process until smooth.

✳ Pour the filling on to the base and bake until the centre is set, about 1 hour. Turn off the oven, prop open the oven door and leave the cake in the oven to cool for 15 minutes. Remove the cake from the oven and cool completely in the pan, about 1 hour.

✳ To make the icing, in a small bowl, combine the yogurt and soured cream and stir to mix well.

✳ To serve, release from the pan, top with a thin layer of the icing and grated chocolate, slice into 8 wedges and divide amongst individual dessert plates. Store covered in the refrigerator for up to 4 days.

Nutritional Analysis per Serving

Calories 373 (Kilojoules 1,568); Total fat 17g; Saturated fat 8g; Protein 13g; Cholesterol 38mg; Carbohydrates 45g; Sodium 267mg; Dietary fibre 1g; Calories from fat 40%

Index

Tips

Resources Guide

The following Jane Fonda video and audio programmes optimally complement Cooking for Healthy Living:

✳ Abs, Buns & Thighs
Two 25-minute low impact aerobic and toning programmes to be used alternately.

✳ Low Impact Aerobics & Stretch
A 25-minute aerobic and 20-minute stretch and relaxation routine.

✳ Total Body Sculpting
Two 25-minute toning workouts to be used alternately.

✳ Favorite Fat Burners
A 50-minute compilation of Jane's favourite aerobic routines, plus her personal 15-minute nutritional programme.

✳ Complete Workout
Thirty-five minutes of low impact aerobics and 35 minutes of full body sculpting and stretching.

✳ Yoga Exercise Workout
A 50-minute, three-part workout of modified yoga postures.

✳ Fitness Walkout Audio
Two hours of energetic music with Jane's motivational guidelines to keep you moving at an aerobic pace.

For a catalogue of Jane Fonda exercise videos and audio cassettes:
✳ Jane Fonda Workout
P.O. Box 22
Lake Oswego, OR 97034, USA

To order The Famine Within video:
✳ Direct Cinema Limited
P.O. Box 10003
Santa Monica, CA 90410, USA
00-1-800 525-0000

For information on obtaining organic produce:
✳ Freshlands Wholefoods
196 Old Street
London EC1V 9FR
0171-250 1708

For information on obtaining organic stone-ground and unbleached flours:
✳ Crowdy Mill
Horbertonford
Totnes, Devon TQ9 7HU
01803-732340

✳ Shipton Mill Ltd
Long Newnton
Tetbury, Glos GL8 8RP
01666-505050

For information on obtaining bison:
✳ North American Bison Cooperative
RR1, Box 162 B
New Rockford, ND 58356, USA
00-1-701 947-2505,
fax 00-1-701 947-2105

For referrals on eating disorder treatment:
✳ Eating Disorders Association
Sackville Place
44 Magdalen Street
Norwich, Norfolk NR3 1JE
01603-621 414

Acknowledgments

For Weldon Owen: Vice President and Publisher: Wendely Harvey; Managing Editor: Jill Fox; Consulting Editor: Norman Kolpas; Recipe Analysis and Nutritional Consultant: Hill Nutrition Associates, Inc; Recipe Writer: Robin Vitetta; Recipe Contributor: Karen Averitt; Eating Disorders Consultant: Janice M. Cauwels, Ph.D; Consultants: Julie LaFond and Nancy Howitt; Editorial Concept: Lu Sierra; Copy Editor: Judith Dunham; Design Concept: John Bull; Designer: Kari Perin; Production Director: Stephanie Sherman; Production Coordinator: Tarji Mickelson; Production Editors: Ruth Jacobson and Janique Gascoigne; Editorial Assistant: Sara Deseran; Proofreaders: Desne Border and Ken DellaPenta; Indexer: ALTA Indexing Service; Illustrator: Jennie Oppenheimer; Recipe Testers: Peggy Fallon and Paul Torgerson; Food Photographer: Joyce Oudkerk Pool; Food Stylist: Pouké; Assistant Food Stylist: Michelle Syracuse; Prop Stylist: Carol Hacker; Photography Assistant: Myriam Varela; Photographer, cover and pages 9, 12 and 20: Firooz Zahedi; Stylists, cover and pages 9 and 12: Chris McMillan (hair), Wayne Massarelli (cover and page 12 makeup), Lutz (page 9 makeup), Linda Medevene (clothing); Photographer, page 11: John Engstead; Photographer, page 28: Rob Lewine; Food Props: American Rag, Cyclamen Studio and Gibson Scheid.